NEW PERSPECTIVES
ON IRELAND

COLONIALISM & IDENTITY

Selected Papers
from the
Desmond Greaves Summer School
and
Related Essays

Introduced & Edited by

Daltún Ó Ceallaigh

To Fionnuala

Ó Dhaltúí

Published by
Léirmheas
P.O. Box 3278, Dublin 6, Ireland,
in conjunction with
The Desmond Greaves Summer School

August 1998

ISBN 0-9518777-6-3

History Politics Literature Economics Science Ireland

Printed from camera-ready copy and bound by
Elo Press Ltd, Dublin, Ireland.

CONTENTS

FURTHER RECONSIDERATIONS

DALTÚN Ó CEALLAIGH

This is the second volume in the reconsiderations series. The first featured: historical and political revisionism in general; colonialism and, on the one hand, language and, on the other, literature; and women's history. In this collection, other facets of Irish history and politics are focused on: initial invasion; the much neglected subject of science and nationality, and revisionism once more, albeit in more specific contexts, such as the Gaelic response to conquest, and the controversial Ulster rising of 1641. The last volume also contained a politico-biographical piece on C Desmond Greaves and this one includes a chapter on Raymond Crotty and his original sociological and economic thought. It ends with a topical and incisive contribution about the north and identity. Indeed, as the subtitle of this book indicates, colonialism and identity, both distinctively and interactively, are the leitmotivs of concern.

Insofar as revisionism is dealt with herein, the contrast is again drawn between the destructive and constructive variety. Both obviously seek to revise our knowledge and understanding of the past as well as the present arising from it. But there is an ongoing difference between those who engage in re-examination with the aim of uplifting and bettering our people and those who strive either to diminish and demoralise, or to be 'novel' with little regard for social and psychological consequences. Ironically, the destructive revisionists often labour towards their object, not just through refusing to ignore or suppress unpleasant or disruptive facts, but by making assumptions or proffering interpretations which are simply unreasonable and, therefore, incredible. The aping, in both tone and attitude, of external, anti-Irish opinion is often evident. In other words, and with an emotional-intellectual symmetry, their mean spiritedness leads them to jaundiced judgements. Brendan Bradshaw, in the last volume of reconsiderations and in this one, has brought out this point with more than one illustration. Of course, not all negative revisionism is to be explained this way. Sometimes what one encounters simply reflects poor work or plain wrong-headedness, and that also has to be dealt with.

The phenomenon continually manifests itself, and never more clearly than when destructive revisionists turn to journalism. Take, for instance, this quotation from Ruth Dudley Edwards: 'the appalling Brendan MacKenna (the Hibernicised version of whose name I do not use since he adopted it late in life only to annoy unionists)'.[†] A more stupid, arrogant, and bigoted statement it would be hard to conceive of. Destructive revisionism thus still ranges from the communal self-deprecation (as distinct from self-critique) of certain insecure cosmopolitans in academe to that sad coterie of embittered anti-nationalists who go to make up the *Sunday Independent* school of Irish history and politics, with its admixture of emeritus, extramural and amateur. It can also involve an attempt at perspicacity which ends up more in self-revelation; what the author puts forward as societal insight is often an unwitting exposure of personal hang-up. This can be seen on occasion either in the would-be sophistication of Fintan O'Toole or the distortional rants of Kevin Myers, both to be found in *The Irish Times*.[*]

[†] *The Irish Times*, 7 July 1998. Breandán MacCionnaith is chairman of the Garvaghy Road Residents' Association.

[*] See, for example, O'Toole's *Opinion* about refugees on 7 August 1998.

Constructive revisionism, or 'reconsiderationism' (rather than mere anti-revisionism), does not call for any sweeping under the carpet of important information or a sensible reading of it. It simply sees no contradiction between commitment and scholarship. Indeed, it views lack of commitment as morally reprehensible, especially when one derives one's livelihood from the people for whom one has so little concern or so much disdain. Commitment can take the form of a deliberate ideological perspective, but it does not have to; all that it requires is that one starts with a criterion of service to the community and proceeds conscientiously from there to investigate and evaluate, letting neither the wish to defend nor fear of offending contaminate method insofar as one can do so. If censures have thus to be made of the nationalist canon, the result, coming from constructive revisionism, and expressed in critical but not scornful terms, should be ultimately to improve and enhance rather than discredit and depress. (Brendan Bradshaw also speaks of 'post-revisionism' in regard to going beyond the historiographical influence of Butterfield.)

But the question today in assessment of issues is not just one of seeing both sides of the story, but spurious moral equivalence. Detachment and balance, fairness and reconciliation, as viewed by some, produce the pseudo-liberal fudge that conflict can be resolved through acknowledging equality of guilt as the obverse of parity of denunciation. The problem that we have to escape from, as John Bruton advises us, is 'the false notion, derived from the French Revolution, that people have inalienable rights.' [†]

[†] *The Irish Times,* 14 July 1998. Mr Bruton's timing was always impeccable.

More than two hundred years of democratic and progressive error have led to the conclusion that some traditions should give way to others. Again by reference to the Garvaghy Road, 'croppies lie down' and 'they shall not pass' are slogans of indistinguishable value. One can imagine the same kind of people in the Thirties trying to have us perceive the well-meaning intentions of fascism, the energizing aspect of nazism. Because we are all human beings, there is no evil. After all, Hitler was some mother's son.

Protestants may possess the light of the Reformation and a vision of civil and religious liberty, but these are not to be separated out from colonialist arrogance and sectarian hatred. Instead, the talk is of Protestant unionist culture which is to be accepted or even celebrated rather than analysed and evaluated. The other of the 'two' traditions is, explicitly or implicitly, Catholic nationalism, although the 'Catholic' may be fading a bit nowadays. Therein, again no distinctions are drawn such as between the heritage of Tone and O'Connell, of Connolly and Griffith. Thus the conservative and reactionary join hands in the name of neighbourliness and good will to stem the enlightenment and advancement of society. Or so they believe, or so their instinct leads them to behave. However, the choice is not just between hibernianism and orangeism; there are other traditions such as republicanism and libertarianism (in their pristine senses). It is the best of those that we should seek to promote and, in order to do so, we must counteract the alternative of an orange-hibernian Janus which obstructs the door to a positive and enriching future.

1. IRELAND - CONQUEST, SETTLEMENT & COLONISATION

A F O'BRIEN

This essay is thematic and is not, therefore, intended to provide a comprehensive account of the political history of late medieval and early modern Ireland. Such is beyond the scope of an essay such as this. Rather, it seeks to explore the general context in which the two English invasions of Ireland, that under the Anglo-Normans from the late twelfth century onwards and that of the sixteenth and early seventeenth centuries, occurred. In this connection, it focuses on the basic elements of Anglo-Irish relations and the emergence of a profound racial antagonism on the part of many Englishmen towards the Irish, a racialism, in short, which both the attitudes of the conqueror and colonist and the conquest itself engendered. The paper consists of a synthesis of the findings of scholars, working in the late medieval and early modern periods, in regard to a range of issues bearing, one way or another, on the question of colonisation, particularly in Ireland, and the attitudes and philosophies conducive to colonisation.

The twelfth and thirteenth centuries witnessed important movements of expansion and colonisation extending from the core areas of western Europe to the European periphery. Thus

> in the centre of the feudalised parts of twelfth century Western Europe the concept of core and periphery was a reality in the minds of people who considered themselves heirs of the civilisation of Latin Christendom. Their economies, based on a long-established urban system, were more highly developed than those at the periphery. This consciousness of superiority was one of the driving

forces of medieval colonisation. It strengthened the idea of crusades and the expansionist tendencies of feudal societies. Set into this wider framework, the colonisation of medieval Ireland takes on a European perspective. It was part of the general process of people moving from the relatively crowded core areas of Western Europe into the more peripheral regions.[1] †

Accordingly

Ireland at the western edge of Europe shared in these developments under similar historical conditions to those experienced by people at the eastern periphery of the medieval core-area of Europe. From the late twelfth century onwards the Anglo-Normans colonised large parts of Ireland while simultaneously the Germans began to colonise the lands of the West Slavic people east of the River Elbe, of the Baltic tribes along the Baltic Sea and the Magyars in the mountainous northern part of their country.[2]

A vibrant feudal socio-economic system was at the heart of this development. Thus, for the most part, this movement of expansion, which had the effect of integrating the newly conquered lands with the old, the core areas of western Europe, 'had, as its characteristic agents, not the powerful monarchies ... but consortia, entrepreneurial associations of Frankish knights, Latin priests, merchants, townsmen and ... peasants.'[3] Furthermore, the western European feudal aristocracy, which inspired the movement, imposed the stamp of their own political and socio-economic organisation on the conquered lands. Thus, 'regions like Ireland, the eastern Baltic, Greece, Palestine and Andalusia, which had not known fiefs, vassals and homage in 1050, became familiar with them in the following centuries.'[4]

---

† References and Notes to this chapter commence on p 175.

The Anglo-Norman invasion of Ireland in the late twelfth century, therefore, must be seen as part of a wider movement of western European colonial expansion. Thus 'Ireland was certainly extensively colonised from England and Wales in the twelfth and thirteenth centuries' and 'that colonisation included the cultivation of new land and in some degree the displacement of the native population.' [5] That phenomenon requires further examination.

'When the Anglo-Normans moved westwards into Wales and Ireland ... they encountered societies which in their eyes were underdeveloped and which they labelled as "barbarian".' [6] Thus 'English literary sources from the later middle ages portrayed the Celt as the perfect barbarian exhibiting all of the characteristics of his savagery - poverty, sloth, incontinence, treachery, brutality, and cruelty.' [7] The development of this attitude reflected profound changes in England.

> For many centuries England and the Celtic world had been very similar societies. But in the course of the tenth, eleventh and early twelfth centuries profound European, economic, social, military and cultural developments affected the south-east of Britain, a wealthy region close to centres of learning, much more rapidly and intensively than they did a remote upland fringe. By the twelfth century this development meant that they had grown sufficiently far apart for the differences to be visible to contemporaries.[8]

In this connection the writings of William of Malmesbury in the twelfth century are particularly important for they gave clear expression to the concepts of 'civilisation' and 'barbarism'. 'As William's ideas were taken up, repeated and elaborated many times over [in the course of the later twelfth century] ... so a new, negative and condescending attitude to Celtic peoples was established, one which was to endure over many centuries.' William's system of classification, therefore, 'divided men and women into the civilised and the barbarians on the basis of the level of their socio-economic development. In the course of British history this was to be the great divide, the creation of an imperialist culture.' [9] By the time of the Anglo-Norman invasion of Ireland ideas such as these were well established and current. Accordingly, condemnation of Irish, Welsh and Scottish societies

> may be said ... to concentrate on three issues. First, these societies were economically underdeveloped and indeed culpably backward. Their agriculture was primitive and pastoral; town life, trade and money were more or less absent; forms of economic exploitation and exchange were primitive. 'The soil of Ireland', as William of Newburgh put it, 'would be fertile, if it did not lack the industry of a capable farmer; but the people are rough and barbarous in their ways ... and lazy in agriculture'. For William - as for so many commentators in generations to come - defects of character were the obvious explanation for economic backwardness. Secondly, these societies [lacking a centralised political authority] were politically immature. ... Thirdly, the social customs and moral, sexual and marital habits of these societies showed they were at best at an early stage of social evolution ... , at worst that 'this barbarous nation', as the Pope had it of the Irish, was 'Christian only in name', and was ... in fact pagan.[10]

Such ideas could be deployed to advantage in the process of conquest and colonisation. Thus

> the perception of Celtic societies as barbarous obviously functioned in part as an ideology of conquest. This is evident from ... the kinds of justification - like the papal bull *Laudabiliter* (forged or not) - which Gerald de Barri [Giraldus Cambrensis or Gerald of Wales] and others put forward to legitimise Henry II's conquest of an island to

which he had no claim of the conventional kind (i.e. based on some alleged hereditary right). ... The greater significance of the imperialist outlook was the barrier it set up between conqueror and conquered - a barrier which inhibited assimilation.[11]

The characterisation of the invasion and conquest of Ireland

as the struggle of 'civilisation' with 'barbarism'. ... was immensely satisfying to advocates of the dominant lifestyle, who thereby assured themselves of their own superiority and of the desirability of the conquest or conversion of their rivals. ... Invariably the Celtic societies were condemned as hopelessly backward and underdeveloped. Feelings of contempt and hostility that were engendered seemed to justify English aggression; and the libel of the Celt ... provided a rationale for various attempts to dominate or annihilate them.[12]

Irish economic inferiority had important military consequences also and English superiority in arms was clearly demonstrated as the invasion and conquest of Ireland progressed. Thus the use of mailed soldiers was itself an indication of socio-economic development and this military supremacy explains why it was the English who were the expansionary power within the British Isles. We have here an unequal struggle between an industrially advanced power and a pastoral economy. ... This too is a measure of the economic transformation which England had undergone - but which Wales and Ireland had not and Scotland only to a very limited extent.[13]

Accordingly

the coming of the Anglo-Normans represented the triumph of a vibrant, confident, aggressive economic mentality which had come to dominate north-western Europe from the second half of the eleventh century. In terms of the exploitation of resources, the marketing of produce, and availability of money as a unit of exchange, the centrality of the town in the exchange and distribution of surpluses and the ability to sustain a ... large and socially - differentiated population the Anglo-Normans surely belonged to a new world. And they knew it.[14]

Accordingly, 'in the protracted struggle of civilization with various kinds of barbarism, the advantage always lay with civilized man. His superiority in numbers and wealth and his more sophisticated systems of communication and control assured his eventual triumph over poorer, diffused, and decentralized societies.' [15]

Apart from socio-economic development, Ireland also differed from the feudalised European core in its ecclesiastical organisation and its marital and sexual mores.

The differences between church organisation and structure in Ireland and that which obtained in the western European core, however, had been narrowed to some degree by a series of church councils held in Ireland in the course of the twelfth century. Nevertheless, this programme had not been completed at the time of the Anglo-Norman invasion. Likewise, Irish marriage law was attacked by church reformers within and without Ireland. As the western church came to control and regulate marriage in the course of the twelfth century, 'Celtic marriage law was now regarded as thoroughly disreputable ... Thus it is not surprising that it should be in the matter of sex and marriage and within the circle of ecclesiastical reformers that we can detect the earliest signs of the approach of a new and hostile attitude to Celtic peoples.' [16] Accordingly, Irish sexual mores and marriage laws increasingly came to be regarded as 'scandalous'.[17] This situation has been described thus

> Celtic Christianity, once so dynamic, expansive, and creative, suffered the effects of prolonged insularity and isola-

tion. The Irish, Scottish and Welsh churches had been by-passed by waves of reformism and revivalism that had energized and transformed the continental and English churches. Institutionally and intellectually the religion of the Celtic peoples was old-fashioned, provincial and impoverished ... Whenever English colonists or conquerors encountered it, however, they denounced such intolerable Celtic deviations as the monastic organization of their churches, the weakness of the diocesan and parochial systems, hereditary benefices, and several clerical vices which reformers had begun to eliminate from the continental and English churches. ... Shortly after the invasion of Ireland by Henry II the council of Cashel was convened to undertake the reformation of the Irish church along English lines and in compliance with the papal mandate *Laudabiliter*, which had called upon Henry and his lieges to extirpate the 'filthy abominations' and 'enormous vices' of the Irish.[18]

Thus the aberrant situation in Ireland was not only criticised by native reformers but was used as a pretext for invasion by the Anglo-Normans. In so doing, however, the invader, clerical or lay,

made a neat elision. For, while twelfth-century Anglo-Norman incursions into Ireland were motivated, in the words of a contemporary source, by the desire for 'land or pence, horses, armour or chargers, gold and silver ... soil or sod', the invaders were able to claim 'some show of religion' by portraying the Irish, in the words of St Bernard, as 'Christians only in name, pagans in fact'.

Therefore, 'when we bear in mind the earlier missionary history of the Irish, the phrase used to justify the planned Anglo-Norman invasion of Ireland is poignant: its purpose was "to expand the boundaries of the Church". Not sharing the social patterns of western Europe meant not being part of the Church.' [19]

The consequences for the Irish were dire. Thus

> although Christianity was ancient in Ireland, the history of the country in the twelfth and thirteenth centuries seems to be marked by processes very similar to those that were taking place in the areas of northern and eastern Europe being incorporated into Latin Christendom at that same time. The incursion of a feudal cavalry élite, the immigration of peasant settlers, the formation of chartered towns, the introduction of a more widely diffused documentary literacy and coinage - all those aspects of Irish history can be paralleled in other areas experiencing the expansionary wave of the High Middle Ages. A colonial settlement in Munster would have a strong resemblance to one in Brandenburg. Ireland ... [was] subject to many of the same processes of conquest, colonization and cultural and institutional transformation as eastern Europe or Spain.[20]

Accordingly, in England, by the twelfth century, Ireland and the other Celtic countries 'were perceived as poor and primitive societies - primitive in that they had failed to climb the ladder of evolution of human societies which twelfth-century intellectuals like Gerald [de Barri or Gerald of Wales] took for granted. By contrast the English saw themselves as prosperous, peaceful, law-abiding, urbanised and enterprising.'[21] It is not without significance that these same arguments were made by the English conquerors and colonisers of Ireland in the later sixteenth and early seventeenth centuries and that, in that context, the works of Gerald of Wales were consulted and his arguments and assertions reiterated. Thus

> in the case of the Irish, the ... history of centuries of half-completed conquest meant that the new attitude of superiority, hostility and alienation was to remain deeply entrenched. English writers of the sixteenth and seventeenth centuries were to do little more than play variations on

themes already well and truly established in Gerald's Irish writings.[22]

Gerald's commentaries on the condition of Ireland at the time of the Anglo-Norman invasion and on the early course of that invasion are particularly important. His role in this regard, it has been argued, was similar to that played by Helmold of Bosau and Otto of Freising 'contemporary continental chroniclers who wrote about the territory of the German colonisation east of the Elbe'.[23] Gerald joined the entourage of Henry II in 1184 and came to Ireland with Henry's son, the future King John, in 1185 and made a third visit in 1199.[24] 'The result of his literary work during 1185 and the following two or three years was his first account of Ireland and its early history, his *History* or *Topography of Ireland*.' [25] Furthermore, 'within twenty years of the coming of the Anglo-Normans to Ireland in 1169 Gerald of Wales had composed his Conquest of Ireland (*Expugnatio Hibernica*) ... As a member of one of the leading families involved in the venture, Gerald could draw on the memories of his uncles and cousins, who had been battling in Ireland for twenty years.' [26]

Gerald's writings reflect both the militaristic, entrepreneurial attitudes of the class to which he belonged, the feudal military aristocracy, and the disparaging, dismissive, even racist, attitude to the Irish to be found in contemporary England.

> Gerald saw the native Irish as typical barbarians, whose life, lived so close to nature, promoted vigour, hardiness, and courage but denied them the 'arts' of civilization. Drawing upon classical ideas about the progress of civilization, he speculated as to the causes of their poverty and backwardness. Unlike most peoples who progressed from pastoralism to agriculture to urban life, the Irish had remained wedded to the pastoral pursuits of their ancestors.

This accounted for their sloth and poverty and for their dependence on imported manufactures. ... Gerald described them as barbarous in every respect. The seclusion of Ireland from the benevolent influence of more advanced societies left them hopelessly and helplessly wrapped in the cocoon of their antiquated and limited way of life.[27]

These attitudes served to engender a sense of mission on the part of the English colonists in later medieval Ireland, the 'English of Ireland', as they called themselves. For example, in a highly charged political situation in 1317, when the very existence of the colony seemed to be in doubt, the colonists pointed to the missionary significance of the invasion.[28] Thus

in 1317 the Gaelic Irish backers of Edward Bruce had sent a justification of their behaviour, which contravened the papal grant of Ireland to Henry II, to Pope John XXII. This document, known to historians as the *Remonstrance of the Irish Princes*, used as part of its argument the crimes committed against the Irish by the English of Ireland.

Apparently, in reaction to that petition, the colonists sent a petition of their own, which 'reads very much like a riposte to the *Remonstrance*', to Edward II.

The petition dwelt upon the anarchic state of Ireland before the arrival of the English, the endowment of the Church by Henry [II] and his successors, and the beneficent role of English law in fostering order. Recent problems, it argued, sprang from the laxness of judges, and especially the failure to exact the death penalty for felonies. In short, it presented the historical role of the English of Ireland as a civilizing mission (of a somewhat rigorous type). They were stimulated to express their sense of the legitimacy of their position by a momentary unease about

18

the Crown's commitment to it. Both the interpretation and the anxiety endured. There was, for instance, an interest in Gerald of Wales's writings, which explained how and why the English of Ireland came to be where they were; and in the early fifteenth century Gerald was to be used in a forlorn effort to attract the attention of the Lancastrian dynasty to their other island and its neglected community.

From the outset of the invasion, Henry II imposed 'the stamp of his own authority on the process of conquest' and claimed 'the overlordship of the whole of Ireland, whether under English or native Gaelic control, for himself.' [29] Ireland, thus, became part of the dominions of the Crown of England and, in 1254, it was stipulated that 'the land of Ireland shall never be separated from the Crown but should remain to the Kings of England forever'. [30]

The conquest of Ireland, however, 'was haphazard, incomplete, and unevenly sustained'. [31] Thus the 'uneven pattern of conquest, control, and settlement meant that [Ireland] in the [later] medieval period [was a society] of multiple and highly localized frontiers ... where two peoples met, overlapped, and confronted each other'. [32] In this respect Ireland had much in common with Wales. Thus

in Ireland and Wales ... alien settlement came ... in the wake of conquest and the English settlers entrenched their position in the host society by institutionalizing the separation between themselves and the native peoples. So it was that the governmental terminology of Wales and Ireland from at least the thirteenth century predicated a duality in the peoples and institutions of both countries ... Such a duality ... sanctioned and promoted a mentality of separation and discrimination which in its turn begat a profound psychological frontier within both countries. A deep and officially sanctioned fissure of race and culture ran through the societies of medieval Wales and Ireland: the attempts, conscious or unconscious, either to deepen or to bridge that fissure were one leading motif in the histories of both countries in the later Middle Ages. Both societies were, in that respect, truly frontier societies.[33]

Though never complete, the English lordship of Ireland, at its peak, was very extensive indeed, and few areas of Ireland were totally unaffected or uninfluenced by the English colony in Ireland.[34] Moreover, an abiding effect of the Anglo-Norman invasion and settlement was that 'in spite of everything - the Gaelic recovery, economic decline, the virtual collapse of royal authority - the fact remains that Ireland would never again be Gaelic in the sense that it had been before 1169.'[35] Because the conquest - partial though it may have been - occurred in economic and demographic circumstances which were profoundly favourable for colonisation and settlement, it had a more profound impact on the Irish economy and polity than the Norman conquest ever had on England. Thus

it seems clear that only when conquest was accompanied by appropriate economic conditions could it sustain a process of colonisation. Had Ireland been conquered by William [duke of Normandy] in 1066, or by Edward I in 1282 [when there was no longer a population surplus available for settlement and colonisation], the character of the ensuing settlement would surely have been fundamentally different from that which actually occurred in 1169. In the long-term Ireland might have emerged as firmly Gaelic as England was to become securely English.[36]

In the attempt made by the English crown and the colonial aristocracy in Ireland to enforce their domination we are witnessing 'a deliberate attempt to bring native society, at the level of leaders and communities alike, more firmly within the authority of lordship and within the ambit of its rules. ... It is a familiar episode of the intensification of the powers of domination in different parts of the world in many different periods.' [37] The thirteenth century was a crucial period in the development of the English medieval lordship. Not only was colonisation and settlement then at its most intense, particularly in the first half of the century, but also in the course of that century 'a shift in attitude seems to take place which makes the language and assumptions of colony more common in the documents of government.' [38] Indeed, it has been argued that 'the middle of the thirteenth century saw a turning-point in many aspects of the history of the colony. It saw the consolidation of the process of imposing on the colony the developed common law of England, a legal system remarkably centralised and remarkably effective as an instrument of royal power by contemporary European standards.' [39] This development may well have been prompted, at least in part, by the fact that, as the thirteenth century progressed, the prospect of complete conquest receded as the invader encountered a 'co-ordinated resistance by the Irish as a people ... as a response to the threat of total domination.' This served to bring about 'the emergence of an awareness of national identity on the part of the subject people.' [40]

The notion of colony was promoted also by the broad thrust of political development in thirteenth century England whereby 'England became a much more politically integrated society and one in which a sense of English national identity and even superiority was cultivated.' Thus 'as the fabric of the political and governmental unity of the English state was more tightly woven, so the relationship of Ireland to the metropolis was construed in political, administrative and legal matters as one of dependence and conformity, so also were the lines of racial division between English and Irish drawn more clearly.' In this way 'the ideology of colony had been defined.' [41]

In these circumstances a policy of racial exclusion soon emerged in the colony underpinned, principally, by the denial of the benefits of English law, the law of the rulers of much of the island, to Irishmen and by attempts to exclude them from ecclesiastical preferment in the areas held and settled by the colonists. 'It appears that from the early thirteenth century the English Crown and its subjects in Ireland sought to implement a policy of deliberate racial exclusion.' [42] Thus, in 1217, the English government directed that Irishmen should not be elected or promoted to sees and dignities when vacant 'as the peace of Ireland has been frequently disturbed by elections of Irishmen'.[43] Thus 'the legal distinction became increasingly the symbol of a "two-nation" mentality, of the entrenching of racial rivalries and of the acceptance of racial categorisations as a datum of social and political life in Ireland.' [44] Again, 'the intensification of racial feeling in the later Middle Ages also involved the growth of a new biological racism. ... In late medieval Ireland ... urban statutes barred the native Irish from town citizenship or guild membership'.[45]

The medieval statutes of the city of Waterford are a case in point. Thus, a statute of 1385, which clearly reflects the English colonial notion that the Irish were racially inferior, prescribed that anyone living in Waterford who insulted a fellow citizen of that city by calling him an Irishman would be obliged to pay 13s 4d by way of compensation to him.[46] Another statute of 1460, which enshrined the principle of English common law that people of Irish blood were in effect bondmen and serfs, declared that no man of Irish blood should be given the freedom of the city of Waterford (such freedom was a prerequisite for anyone wishing to engage in trade or to practise a craft within the city) without first obtaining his freedom and liberty, i.e. a grant to him of English law, from the king of England together with his manumission (a grant of freedom) from the lord to whom he was bound.[47] This provision was further extended in 1466 when it was ordained that Irishmen might not be received into the franchise and liberty of Waterford simply by way of marriage to a citizen or freeman of the city; such admission henceforward would need the consent of the corporation.[48] A statute of 1470 further extended these provisions by stipulating that any apprentice or any other person of Irish blood living in Waterford who wished to enjoy the benefit of the liberty and franchises of the city should first obtain his freedom from the king of England and then dress in the English manner and speak English.[49]

Yet, despite statutes of this kind, designed to mark off the English nation from the Irish (in this respect, as much as anything else, the statutes were defensive in character), persons of Irish blood were to be found in the towns, not least the major seaport trading towns of the colony. The plain fact of the matter is that in practice there was a symbiotic relationship between Gaelic Ireland and the English lordship.[50] Thus

> while advantageous to Gaelic Ireland, trade between it and the lordship was essential for the prosperity of many of the merchants of the towns of the colony. Some of the latter, it should be emphasised, were Gaelic Irish in origin who, by means of grants of denization,[51] enjoyed the benefits of English law which permitted them to engage in trade in the king's dominions and to secure their interests in English law. ... Evidently in response to changing conditions and new needs, as the fifteenth century progressed, such grants of denization became more common. Consequently, the racial composition of the towns of the lordship became even more mixed and, we can assume, ties with Gaelic Ireland were strengthened. The situation had thus radically changed from that which had obtained in the thirteenth and fourteenth centuries when attempts had

been made to prevent Irishmen from being appointed to ecclesiastical benefices or to public or civil office in the towns.

The growth of racial attitudes of the kind described above marked off the Gaelic Irish from the English of Ireland and prevented the fusion of the two races. Thus the development of a sense of national or ethnic superiority on the part of English settlers in Ireland in the course of the thirteenth and early fourteenth centuries sharpened the effects of conquest which increasingly was seen by the Gaelic Irish as 'much more than a military take-over; it had led, sooner or later, to the establishment of a regime in which the line between vanquished and victor was that between discrimination and privilege. ... It was the mentality of men who regarded themselves as both so superior and so insecure that their status must be defended by privilege.' [52]

Notwithstanding the tensions between the two races in later medieval Ireland there was significant cultural and economic interaction between them. This has already been noted in the case of the towns of the English colony, but it existed also at other levels of colonial society. The attitudes of the Anglo-Irish aristocracy and even important elements of the colonial gentry, who wielded so much power in late medieval Ireland, testify strongly to this development. Thus our attention has been directed to the 'growing interest shown by Anglo-Irish magnates in Gaelic pseudo-history and genealogy',[53] partly in response to changes in the political conditions obtaining in the English lordship of Ireland in the later middle ages and partly because of the growing intellectual respectability of the schools of native Irish learning in the eyes of many of the colonists. It has been argued that

it was this intellectual respectability that caused the Anglo-Irish to turn to the study of pseudo-history when they
felt a need to validate their titles in the fifteenth century.
As the area of royal control contracted to the four counties
round Dublin, it was not enough for the earls and barons
ruling beyond the Pale to appeal to feudal tenure or a
charter from the king as the basis of their authority. They
were anxious to be proclaimed as heirs, by right of conquest, to the dues and boundaries of specific pre-Norman
kingdoms, and as mystical husbands of the territories they
now ruled by virtue of their strength and justice. This was
no rejection of the English king's authority, it was simply
becoming irrelevant. ... By the late sixteenth and early
seventeenth centuries this desire to be accepted as fully
Irish had accelerated. The word *Éireannach* or 'Ireland-
man' was coined ...

The Renaissance and the Counter-Reformation [gave]
rise to new concepts of patriotism that were to find their
fullest expression in the literature and politics of the seventeenth century. But the roots of this change go back to
the fifteenth century, and each stage in its development
has been articulated for us through the services of the native poets and historians, who from time immemorial were
trained and paid to clothe aspirations in words.[54]

Certainly by the late middle ages the English of Ireland
felt very insecure as the colony was troubled by political and
economic adversity. Accordingly, while regarding the Irish
as their 'natural enemies' and strongly asserting their
Englishness, they nevertheless identified with Ireland and, in
particular, they took pride in their history as settlers in it
and, in so doing, they marked themselves off, in important
respects, from the metropolitan English.[55] The Statutes of
Kilkenny of 1366, therefore, served a twofold purpose. First,
'to erect a wall, broken only by official crossing points,
between the English and the Irish' and, second, 'to uproot

the fence that mutual jealousies were threatening to build between the settlers and those who sailed from England to their rescue.' [56]

The polity of late medieval Ireland was exceedingly complex. Thus English Ireland by the fifteenth century consisted of the following elements: (1) the area commonly called the Pale which consisted of a relatively small area centred on Dublin, 'which still followed the English common law and recognised the jurisdiction of the Dublin courts';[57] (2) the great Anglo-Irish feudal lordships which owed nominal allegiance to the English crown but, in practice, were autonomous; (3) the seaport towns which were increasingly subjected to the pressure of feudal lords, to distress due to political disturbance and to economic malaise.[58] The remainder of the island was in the hands of various Gaelic Irish rulers. There was, however, considerable interaction between the two races. There were strong trading contacts, and Gaelic Irish were to be found not only in the great feudal lordships, but even in the Pale and the seaport towns. These contacts did much to diminish, or at least to overcome to some degree, the long-standing tensions between the two races, which, in any event, were unable to displace each other. The fifteenth century, however, saw the growth of anti-Irish sentiment in England which could be directed as much against the English of Ireland as the Gaelic Irish.

Not only were there striking political differences within Ireland, but economic conditions varied also. Gaelic Ireland differed greatly from the western European norm in regard to settlement and economy. While there was some production of cereals, particularly oats, the economy of Gaelic Ireland was largely pastoral being based, largely, on cattle production. By contrast, economic and social conditions in the Pale were not unlike those obtaining in parts of England. Outside the Pale, in the earldom of Ormond for example, some areas continued to be organised on a manorial basis. It is, therefore, difficult to generalise about economic conditions, but we can say with certainty that much of late medieval Ireland was economically underdeveloped. Therefore, in regard to both political and economic organisation, Ireland, at the outset of the sixteenth century, was inferior to England.

At the end of the middle ages Ireland was culturally divided, politically fragmented and economically underdeveloped. Accordingly, it was dangerously open to English conquest which, as English interests dictated and English economic, demographic and social conditions permitted, was finally effected in the later sixteenth and early seventeenth centuries. This development marked the fourth wave of invasion of Ireland in historical times and formed part of the general wave of late medieval and early modern European expansion in the Atlantic.

In the period of the Hundred Years' War (1338-1453) the ambitions of English kings had been concentrated on France. Even in the early years of the reign of Henry VIII considerable sums were spent on futile wars in France, perhaps as much as one million pounds in the period 1511 to 1514, while it has been estimated that the total cost of England's wars with France and Scotland in the period 1511 to 1547 amounted to £2,134,784.[59] Ireland continued to be what it had been throughout the late medieval period, peripheral to the main concerns of English monarchs. By the 1530s, however, the English crown's 'awareness of its Irish problem had greatly intensified, while, concurrently, long-term developments outside Ireland substantially altered its perspectives on the problem.' [60]

It has been pointed out that after 1534 English policy regarding Ireland began to envisage the necessity for a thorough conquest of Ireland to be secured by 'colonisation by new English settlers either on a local or a national basis. At its most extreme it called for the clearing of the Irish out of Ireland and their replacement by Englishmen.' [61] Thus 'Tudor conciliation in Ireland - the policy that marked the closing years of the reign of Henry VIII - gave way to Tudor conquest.' [62] Thus English interventionist policies in Ireland developed in the course of the sixteenth century. Whereas in the 1540s and 1550s colonisation appears to have been limited in scale, by the end of the century the earlier policy of conciliating the Gaelic Irish rulers by bringing them into a feudal relationship with the English crown and by demonstrating to them the advantages to be gained from 'civility', the adoption of English culture and institutions, had been abandoned in favour of a more robust approach, one which entailed total conquest and large scale plantation. 'The establishment of small English colonies in the underdeveloped and underpopulated lands of Gaelic Ireland was seen as a means of demonstrating to the Gaelic lords just how profitable the adoption of English social and economic customs could be.' This, however, was but one element in English government policy for

> the government's determination to carry out reform, if necessary by means of coercion, was revealed, not in its somewhat half-hearted interest in colonization, but in its more persistent concern to establish military garrisons in the country. In the 1540s and 1550s attempts to erect garrisons were confined to what were considered to be key strategic sites, in the midlands, on the borders of the Pale and along the southern coastline which was vulnerable to foreign invasion. Under Elizabeth, however, the need for a greater, if more dispersed, military presence became apparent.[63]

In its early phases, therefore, English colonisation in Ireland did not necessarily entail either large-scale plantation or the total removal of the Gaelic Irish. In some cases, however, Gaelic Irish were not to be granted lands under plantation schemes. Thus

> the first effort at a midlands plantation ... was begun ... by St Leger ... who issued the first leases for attainted lands in 1550. The 1550 scheme ... was to remain exclusive to English and Anglo-Irish planters. ... St Leger's involvement in this first (and ultimately abortive) plantation project was not inconsistent. He himself had shown an interest in a number of smaller schemes; but personal considerations apart, settlements of this kind were a valuable support to his general policy. They were strategically necessary in certain difficult or vulnerable areas, and politically important as an exemplary reminder to the Irish lords that the crown expected them to take seriously the obligations which they assumed under the Irish kingdom. But they were more valuable finally as an example to neighbouring natives of the material and cultural benefits which were to be derived from the adoption of English laws and customs which they were now being persuaded to undertake.[64]

Similarly, the earl of Sussex as viceroy in 1556 set himself the task of re-establishing the plantation in Laois-Offaly in the face of rebellion by the O'Mores and O'Connors.[65]

There was, therefore, considerable resistance by the Gaelic Irish to colonisation schemes of this kind.

> The concept of colonization - by which was meant the establishment of planned nucleated settlements of Englishmen - was alien to the Gaelic population of the country ... they knew that ... annihilation faced them if they did not confront the new challenge that was being presented them by the English in Ireland. This understanding did not inspire the Gaelic chieftains to present a united

front against a common foe, but individual Gaelic poets exhorted their particular patrons to emulate the example of their ancestors in keeping the foreigners at bay. Failure to do so, it was claimed, would result in the extinction of their name and kindred from their ancestral lands; to this extent the Gaelic poets revealed an understanding of what the English were about.[66]

Large-scale colonisation by means of plantation, before the late sixteenth century, was impeded also by forces other than Gaelic Irish resistance.

> The subjection of extensive stretches of Irish land to plantation was from the beginning rendered impracticable by the government's unwillingness to countenance it in any meaningful way. Thus despite the broad terms in which colonial grants were commonly framed, the actual projects necessarily assumed a restricted and defensive character because of the crown's refusal to support the wholesale clearance of the native population which a more ambitious undertaking would have required.[67]

A policy of colonisation by means of plantation had taken firm root in Ireland by the 1570s and plantation projects were urged both by Palesmen, the English of Ireland, and by English-born officials.[68] Thus

> innovations had certainly taken place in the process of colonisation between the 1540s and the early 1570s. But the changes that occurred concerned not the theory of colonisation nor its ultimate objective, but the way in which attempts were made to establish them. The phases through which colonising practice passed were closely determined by the general character of the administration under which individual colonial projects were undertaken.[69]

From the 1570s onwards a sustained policy of plantation in Ireland emerged, a policy which reached its ultimate expression in the Plantation of Munster, following the defeat of the earl of Desmond's rebellion in 1583, and the Plantation of Ulster, following the end of the Nine Years' War and the collapse of Gaelic power in that province.[70] With these developments Ireland came fully under English domination and the Gaelic order was at an end.

The policy of the military suppression of Gaelic Ireland to be followed by the colonisation of extensive tracts of Gaelic Irish territory increasingly came to the fore in the period between 1543, when the policy of conciliating the Gaelic Irish rulers was abandoned, and 1565, when Sir Henry Sidney, a prominent exponent of colonisation,[71] was appointed lord deputy of Ireland. It would appear that between those two dates a shift in social thinking had taken place in England. It has been argued that English thinking had evolved to the point that, inspired by the model of imperial Spain and its treatment of the native Indian population in the Spanish colonies, there now existed in England a mature ideology of colonisation. Thus 'the Irish were ... categorised as the most barbarous of peoples, and Englishmen argued that it was their duty and responsibility to hold them down by force so that through subjection they could achieve liberty.'[72] This, it is suggested, marked a major change in attitude on the part of English administrators since 'the old concept of the Irish as socially inferior [in the matter of economic and social organisation] to the English was being replaced with the idea that they were culturally inferior and far behind the English on the ladder of development.'[73] As we have seen, however, ideas such as these go back at least to the twelfth century, particularly to the writings of Gerald de Barri or Gerald of Wales. Thus Gerald's *Expugnatio Hibernica*

> survives in fifteen medieval manuscripts (excluding excerpts) and in the fifteenth century was translated into

both English and Irish, the English version circulating quite widely in Ireland (six manuscripts). The work clearly continued to serve as a popular origin tale for the colony. Indeed, in the translation included in the revised version of Holinshed's *Chronicles* in 1587, it maintained this function into the Elizabethan and Stuart periods.[74]

In all probability, English antagonism towards the Irish, leading to a total contempt for and dismissal of Irish culture and society, was due to no small degree to the intensification of English involvement in Ireland as the sixteenth century progressed ('Ireland was "the moving frontier" of Elizabethan expansion overseas' [75]), to significant resistance on the part of Gaelic rulers necessitating increased military expenditure by the English government, to the enhanced prospect of profit from the exploitation of Irish natural resources which presented itself in the course of the century and, not least, to the strong racial sentiment which developed in contemporary England. These conditions promoted the development of attitudes of English cultural and social superiority vis-à-vis the Gaelic Irish to which Canny refers. Indeed, at times, even the English of Ireland were regarded as inferior to the English-born. These developments, therefore, warrant further examination.

As we have seen, as early as the twelfth century some Englishmen were already imbued with a sense of English cultural superiority. This sentiment strengthened in the course of the late middle ages. Fifteenth-century England saw a steady growth in national consciousness, sharpened particularly by protracted war with France. 'The sixteenth century was a watershed in English history. The Henrician reforms transformed a nation and compelled Englishmen to take a new look at their past.' [76] This entailed 'the antiquarian search for a non-Roman church'. From this emerged an 'anti-French bias which was a feature of the new-found pride in Saxon origins'.[77] A strong, vibrant racial consciousness, not least one infused with myth, could and did degenerate into open racialism, directed against not only Irishmen but foreigners in general. In this connection it is interesting to note the way in which in sixteenth-century England foreigners were blamed for economic problems and difficulties.[78]

Racialism of this kind could flower in appropriate circumstances and lend itself to the ideology of nascent colonialism. This ideology became particularly important in Ireland from the later sixteenth century onwards as the policy of colonisation gathered momentum. The Gaelic Irish were seen as being not merely culturally inferior to the English, but veritable barbarians akin in their status to pagans and American Indians. The corollary to this view of the Irish was the developing notion of the superiority of 'England over all other nations, even the ancient Romans, on the ground that bondsmen were by the sixteenth century virtually unknown in England.' [79] Theories of this kind rested on the assumption that the character of its socio-economic organisation determined the level of civilisation attained by any people. These ideas, by the sixteenth century, as we have seen, were not entirely new. At heart they were racist and, as had been the case in the later middle ages, they were particularly useful weapons in the armoury of a coloniser.

In stating the matter thus, however, it is important to emphasise that there were important differences between sixteenth-century English observers of the Gaelic Irish in their evaluation and analysis just as Gaelic Ireland itself was not monolithic and unaffected in important respects by contact with English administrators and colonists. Thus, it has been argued, doubt must be cast on the existence of a colonial consensus among the New English of Elizabethan Ireland. Certainly Edmund Spenser's *A View of the Present State of Ireland* cannot now be regarded as the classic expression of such a viewpoint - which can only be to the benefit of the historical reputation of the colonists. In the shortrun, in any case, it would seem preferable methodologically to explore the tensions within the colonial ethos rather than search for a dubious consensus. It is only in the light of the tensions that a more basic agreement, if such existed, can be perceived. Furthermore, it must now be clear that the intellectual history of the colony cannot be understood in isolation from the intellectual history of the metropolis. Recent studies of the former have proceeded on the basis that the colonists' response to the Irish experience can be - and ought to be - understood by reference to the content of that experience alone. On the contrary ... perceptions of the Irish reality were conditioned by attitudes and values, philosophies and world-views, acquired in the course of an English upbringing.[80]

Equally, 'Gaelic Ireland was changing dramatically in the sixteenth century not only as a result of internal developments but also because of the way in which the presence of English law and settlements were permeating the traditional structures and ideology of Gaelic society.'[81]

The English colonisers of Ireland and, later, America perceived themselves to be

assisting in the development of a concept of historical process and cultural development, as the widening of the horizons of the articulate citizen of sixteenth-century England, both intellectually and geographically, slowly eroded the old idea of a static world. It was only natural that the aggressive men who sought their fortunes in Ireland should try to fit Gaelic society into their expanding world view. But what provided Englishmen with a growing confidence and pride spelled disaster for Gaelic Ireland which was now seen as a cultural throwback that must be painfully dragged to modernity.[82]

So persuaded of their own superiority and Gaelic Irish inferiority,

> Englishmen produced a moral and civil justification for their conquest of Ireland. Although most of the colonizers avowed that their long-term purpose was to convert the Irish to Christianity, they made no effort to accomplish this end, contending that conversion was impossible so long as the Irish persisted in their barbarous way of life. All were agreed that their immediate object should be the secular one of drawing the Irish to civility.[83]

Seen in this light, the conclusion was readily arrived at that the Irish 'needed to be made bondsmen to enlightened lords who would instruct them in the ways of civil society.' [84] Furthermore, the new ideology was advantageous also in that it held the Irish to be responsible for their condition

> since their heathenism was owing not to a lack of opportunity but rather to the fact that their system of government was antithetical to Christianity. Once it was established that the Irish were pagans, the first logical step had been taken toward declaring them barbarians. The English were able to pursue their argument further when they witnessed the appearance of the native Irish, their habits, customs, and agricultural methods.[85]

The emergence of a sustained policy of plantation in Ireland in the 1570s marked not only an important stage in Irish history but in that of North America also. Irish history in the sixteenth and seventeenth centuries contained 'at least three novel elements: cultural conflict of unprecedented bitterness; religious cleavage; and a palpable hardening of

English administrative policy.' [86] The Elizabethan conquest and colonisation of Ireland should 'be viewed in the wider context of European expansion' since that pattern of conquest and settlement 'was contemporaneous with and parallel to the first effective contacts of Englishmen with North America, to plans for conquest and settlement there, and to the earliest encounters with its Indian inhabitants.' [87] The ideology of cultural and racial inferiority, so diligently applied in North America by the colonialists, first evolved in the Irish context. 'We find colonists in the New World using the same pretexts for the extermination of the Indians as their counterparts had used in the 1560s and 1570s for the slaughter of numbers of the Irish.' [88]

Nonetheless, there were obvious differences between the Gaelic Irish and the North American Indians. Accordingly

> the literature devoted to the reform of the Irish [reflected the fact] that the problems that existed in Ireland presented those who would ponder them with an altogether greater intellectual challenge than did the question of the assimilation of the American Indians. The Indians, or at least the tribes that the English encountered, could plausibly be portrayed as primitives, and those who wished to denigrate them had little difficulty in persuading themselves and their readers that they were dealing with a wicked people who might only be brought to an acceptable mode of existence by force and compulsion. So too with the Gaelic Irish, a people who had been consistently portrayed by English authors as primitive and perverse ever since Giraldus Cambrensis had first depicted them as such. The images of Cambrensis were readily recalled by those who wrote of the Irish in the sixteenth and seventeenth centuries, and it was ominous for both the Irish and the American Indians that authors frequently made cross-cultural references, thereby implying that the two were

descended from the same primitive ancestors or that they were at the same retarded state of cultural development.

To this extent, the literary treatment accorded the Gaelic Irish was as crude and simplistic as that devoted to the American Indians ... In the case of the Indians (and in the case also of the Gaelic Irish) there was little difficulty in persuading the responsible authorities in England that they were dealing with a people who had always been barbaric and that their barbarism could be accounted for by tracing their ancestry to known barbaric tribes in the antique past. Thus it was frequently claimed that the Gaelic Irish were descended from the ancient Scythians who had once lived about the Caspian Sea, and some were at pains to trace their migration across Europe to their eventual settlement in Ireland.[89]

Thus

almost every promoter of English settlement in Ireland, whether in state-sponsored plantations or private colonization, compared their work to that of those contemporaries who were attempting to settle among the North American Indians. Both efforts, it was alleged, were concerned primarily with the advancement of true religion among a heathen or heathenish people; both were concerned with the substitution of civil standards for barbarous customs; and both were intended to promote the enrichment of England through the cultivation of crops or the exploitation of resources that were not available at home. And in developing these comparisons the various writers did not minimize the hazards involved, as when Fynes Moryson advised that 'no less cautions were to be observed' by those engaged in the proposed plantation of Ulster 'than if these new colonies were to be led to inhabit among the barbarous Indians.'[90]

From the outset private interests had been involved in schemes for plantation. This had the advantage of establishing colonies without any cost to the crown.[91] For a government experiencing severe financial pressure from monetary inflation and the soaring costs of government in general and war in particular, this approach, apparently strongly espoused by Sir Henry Sidney, was particularly attractive and made the policy of colonisation especially cogent. If, however, the crown could use private predatory interests to its advantage, those same interests could likewise make use of the royal government. Thus 'like their counterparts in Virginia the new landed proprietors [in Ireland] gained control of the central government but used it as an instrument for their own enrichment rather than for the advancement of the interests of the monarch.'[92] Serving officials in Ireland, therefore, could see

> their primary purpose in Ireland as being one of advancing their own interests rather than those of the Crown. The fact that they could argue that one interest served the other and that every attack on the native society was for the greater benefit of civility reveals the extent to which they had become (and saw themselves to have become) colonists rather than administrators. ... The failure of the English government to intervene decisively to uphold the interests of the community against the incursions of self-seeking officials is partly explained by its increasing preoccupation with the struggle against the might of Catholic Spain. This preoccupation did not result, however, in a corresponding disregard for communal welfare in England and Wales, which suggests that there were other factors besides the threat of Spain to account for a growing official disinterest in Ireland. The most potent of these factors was probably the impatience of the English government with the continued attachment of the Irish population (including the Old English of the Pale) to Catholicism.[93]

Accordingly, 'once Ireland came to be treated differently from England, it in turn provided a model for the management of those transoceanic territories that were soon to come under the control of the English government.' [94]

Two prominent representatives of this group of self-serving officials were Richard Boyle, created earl of Cork in 1622, and Sir John Clotworthy, first viscount Masserene whose careers 'illustrate the usefulness of guile, office and place in building an Irish estate.' [95] Boyle who 'was a typical adventurer, the younger son of a younger son, an orphan without connections' [96] by taking service under the English crown in Ireland and by manipulating his office to his advantage 'was merely the most successful of a crowd of young men, English, Old English and Irish similarly engaged.' [97]

It will be noted from the above that some of those who acquired properties carved out from forfeited lands were Gaelic Irish. Indeed, under the new order Gaelic Irish peasants could gain also. Thus

> those who stood to benefit most from these changes, at least in the short term, were the Irish peasants, who found themselves in a more powerful position to negotiate an improvement in their social and economic conditions than ever before. The fact that they were few in number in the aftermath of the war (when the total population of the country might have been as low as 750,000) was certainly in their favour, but so also was the influx of British proprietors, who were no less anxious than the native landowners to establish tenants on their recently established properties and had no scruples over luring away tenants from their traditional landlords by the simple offer of more favourable terms. These factors resulted in a general erosion of the customary dependency of Irish tenants upon their overlords, and many Irish tenants took advantage of the opportunity to enter into contractual relations with recently appointed English or Scottish landlords. Once these arrangements were engaged upon, the British landlords

were always anxious to prevent their tenants (whether British or Irish) from being lured away by neighbouring lords, and the rivalry and competition that ensued sometimes resulted in physical attacks and attempts to disrupt the law reminiscent of the violence that had characterized relations between neighbouring lords in the society that had just been overthrown. Thus while it could be said that Irish tenants were being brought into an environment which would facilitate their uplift and improvement, it could equally well be said that the newly appointed British landlords were, like the Anglo-Normans before them, succumbing to the culture of the Gaels.[98]

'Gaelic poets ... castigated those who broke with traditional loyalties, but in doing so they sometimes acknowledged there could be economic advantage for those who sided with the English.'[99] In some cases contact with the new British landed proprietors could result in some degree of anglicisation, but, equally,

> cultural influences could also come into play in the opposite direction. For example, British landlords, or at least their agents, saw the need to become conversant in the Irish language so that they could negotiate directly with their Irish tenants, and British tenants also seem to have acquired some knowledge of the language spoken by their Irish neighbours.[100]

The fact is that 'in the case of Ireland ... strictly segregated enclaves of settlers never came into being.'[101]

As already indicated, many of the colonists had little or no interest in 'civilising' the native Irish and were intent only on securing economic advantage and maximising their profits. Some examples of this have already been cited, but some further observations about economic developments would be appropriate at this juncture.

The conquest and colonisation and the process whereby they were effected altered the population of Ireland both in its composition and in its size. There was, of course, significant English and Scottish migration into Ireland. The consequent increase in population, however, was to some degree at least offset by the losses sustained in time of war, notably the Desmond rebellion and the Nine Years' War, and by a Catholic exodus in the aftermath of English Protestant conquest. Thus, for example, expatriate Catholic Irishmen were to be found among the merchant communities of Nantes and Bordeaux in the seventeenth century.[102]

In economic terms, the new order had both positive and negative effects. Some of the positive changes, however, must be seen in context. Thus while the Irish economy became more commercialised in the late sixteenth and seventeenth centuries, this was due, at least in part, to contemporary developments in Europe as a whole. Moreover, in the late fifteenth and early sixteenth centuries the Irish economy was already showing signs of renewal and significant growth in some sectors.[103] Moreover, the attitudes of some of the colonists were more conducive to despoliation than conservation of natural resources. The fact is that 'the picture which had been presented by Giraldus in the *Topographia* of an Ireland where "the land is fruitful and rich in its fertile soil and plentiful harvests" had been more than confirmed by the sixteenth-century descriptions of the island.'[104] Particularly important in this connection were fisheries, both sea and inland, and woodlands.

In 1567, for example, the English 'privy council was deluged by a wide variety of schemes.' Thus 'a plan to farm the fishing of the south and south-east coasts which involved the confiscation of much coastal land in Desmond was entertained'.[105] Again, in east Ulster, for example, the wealth of the agricultural land was considerably supplemented by other natural resources, the fishing and the woods. The significance of the fishing was stressed by at least one tract of the early seventeenth century which highlighted the economic significance of the salmon of the Bann and claimed that there was cod and ling in Lough Neagh. The Bann salmon fishings had been recognised from at least the fifteenth century when Bann salmon was exported to Bristol and during the sixteenth century there had been attempts to exploit the fishing rights of the river by leasing them to farmers. The first of these grants was made to John Travers in 1536 but because of his failure to pay the crown rent the fishing rights were granted in 1571 to Henry Piers of Carrickfergus. Since the Bann itself was de facto in the hands of the O'Neill family for most of the sixteenth century it was difficult to make any real attempt to exploit the fisheries and lessees were reluctant to pay rent for only sporadic control of them. In the early seventeenth century conveyancing problems with the Bann fishing rights drew attention to the economic importance of the royal claim to the fishings which resulted in a series of inquisitions in 1619 into royal fishing rights in east Ulster and the important salmon rights of north Antrim and Belfast were granted to the earl of Antrim, the main landholder in north Antrim, and Sir Arthur Chichester.[106]

Plainly the colonists were intent on exploiting both inland and sea fisheries, although 'the exploitation of the inland fisheries by the settlers was ... resented by the native landowners, who had always appreciated their value.' [107] As already noted 'many early seventeenth-century settlers regarded Ireland as an attractive source of short-term profit and attempted to establish industrial concerns there.' Accordingly, 'Sir Thomas Roper, later Lord Baltinglass, began his Irish career by setting up profitable fisheries at Schull, Crookhaven and Bantry.' [108]

Ireland had exported timber to England and continental Europe in the thirteenth century and these exports were renewed with increasing volume in the late fifteenth and early sixteenth centuries.[109] Much of the timber exported went to ports in the English West Country. Ireland's timber resources, therefore, were well known in England, as indeed, were Irish fisheries and their value. Indeed, 'one of the inducements used to persuade settlers to come to Ireland at the end of the sixteenth century was the profits offered by the exploitation of the woods.'[110] It is not surprising, therefore, to find merchants from south-west England acquiring land under the Munster Plantation, for example in the Youghal area. Therefore, 'from the outset, English merchants, especially those from the western ports, displayed interest in Irish plantations with a view to exploiting the natural resources, especially timber, of the country.'[111] Demand for timber increased steadily in the late fifteenth and sixteenth centuries as both commercial and military needs increased. Thus

> hardwood was in keen demand everywhere in Europe, and the softer woods were used either for pipe staves, which were exported in enormous quantities from Ireland to southern Europe and to the wine islands of the Atlantic, or for the smelting of pig iron, which was imported from England to be processed close to the Irish forests. The ready availability of cash from these endeavours acted as a wonderful stimulus for the British settlers, who set out to strip the country of its trees without any thought for domestic needs in future or for the conservation of the environment.[112]

Accordingly

> the timber trade ... grew particularly rapidly in the early seventeenth century but it was to be a short-lived phenomenon. By the late 1630s the best timber, that used for

pipestaves, was almost exhausted. Areas such as the Bann valley in Ulster, the Slaney valley in south Leinster, the Blackwater and Bandon valleys in Munster were rapidly denuded of timber. ... This dramatic change reflects the 'asset stripping' character of the new order. The management of timber resources in Ireland contrasts strongly with the case in England where conservation and replacement of what was then an almost exhausted resource took priority.[113]

Of course, some woodland was cleared for agricultural purposes and for settlements, but the scale of the clearances and the short period of time in which they occurred suggest massive despoliation. For example, the Dufferin in south Down

> one of the most economically important wooded areas in the sixteenth century had been cleared by 1640 leaving only scrub of little value. By 1640 the only area where any timber of real value remained was on the east shore of Lough Neagh, an area which was settled late and never fully developed before the outbreak of war in 1641.[114]

Again, by agreement between the crown and the City of London Companies in 1610, the woods of Glenconkeyne and Killetra were granted to the City of Derry in perpetuity provided that timber felled in the woods 'would be used for building and other necessary purposes in Ireland.' The Companies, however, seeking to maximise their profits by fully exploiting resources at their disposal, broke the agreement by felling vast quantities of timber to be exported as pipe staves.[115] Similarly, Richard Boyle, earl of Cork, who bought the lands which Raleigh had acquired under the Munster Plantation for £1,500, 'used their timber both in his ironworks and for stave-making. In his diaries Boyle recorded transactions involving about 4,000,000 staves (approximately 500,000 cubic ft) between 1616 and 1628.'[116]

In despoiling the woodlands thus, however, the colonists

could claim to be advancing a civilizing mission because the Irish woods had always been used to advantage by the native forces in the sixteenth century, while in the seventeenth they provided a secure refuge for those erstwhile native soldiers, known as 'raparees' or 'tories', who had no place in the newly planted communities but who took revenge for their loss of status by launching raids upon the settlers. The promoters of timber processing could also claim to be promoting manufacturing employment, and forges, like towns and bridges, were accepted as symbols of the new civil order.[117]

The stated purpose of the English conquest and settlement of Ireland in the sixteenth and early seventeenth centuries was to bring Ireland into conformity with England by establishing a model kingdom in Ireland. Yet, the effects of this policy were to reduce Ireland to colonial status since 'the very means by which the kingdom was fulfilled were the means by which the island's indigenous organs were eradicated and an exogenous elite implanted.'[118] Thus Ireland became 'a unique example of a territory which was colonised in the twelfth and thirteenth centuries in a feudal setting and was recolonised in the sixteenth and seventeenth centuries in a post-feudal setting.'[119] Accordingly, the policy of plantation in Ireland marks 'the first phase of modern English imperialism'[120] and occurred in the wider context of 'English overseas movement which was leading English ships to challenge the ocean monopoly of Spain and Portugal and to make the first tentative attempts to settle colonies in North America.'[121]

Any explanation of the policy of plantation in Ireland necessitates some consideration of basic ·socio-economic developments in England from the later sixteenth century onwards. Prominent among these developments were a marked rise in population and a steady rise in monetary inflation, the burden of which was borne by the wage-earning class; these developments were accompanied by a striking growth in the prosperity of the yeoman class which 'consolidated its position at the heart of English rural society'.[122] In these circumstances there was a considerable growth in both rural and urban poor, as land was concentrated in fewer hands, with a corresponding growth in the food market where inflation drove prices upwards. Accordingly, later sixteenth century England was a land replete with a surplus population (it has been calculated that the population rose from 2½ million in the mid-fifteenth century to five million by 1620) [123] and agitated by much disaffection. There was, therefore, a surplus population available for transportation to new colonial settlements and every reason for the authorities to remove disaffected elements overseas.

In the colonisation of Ireland this factor was particularly important. The plain fact is that in order to secure and consolidate the fruits of military victory it was necessary to underpin conquest by significant settlement. That, in turn, required the availability of a surplus population which could be transplanted to the new settlements. In this respect demographic conditions had been favourable in the twelfth and thirteenth centuries and they were so again in the late sixteenth and seventeenth centuries. Matters, however, were quite different in the fourteenth and fifteenth centuries and that was one of the factors promoting the decline of the English lordship of Ireland in the late middle ages. Thus 'it was necessary to follow up successful warfare with significant settlement buttressed by some measure of military occupation and, for both financial and demographic reasons, that simply was not possible in the bleak conditions of the fourteenth century.' [124]

Conditions in late sixteenth-century England, therefore, encouraged attacks on foreigners, and xenophobic sentiments were deliberately fostered by the crown during the reign of Elizabeth in order 'to muster some national feeling behind herself' in view of the fact that she was 'under the threat of Catholic claimants to the throne, and at war through all the latter part of her reign.' [125] Again, profound social and economic change in England in the sixteenth century produced psychological or philosophical changes also. Thus

> the radical changes in the social and economic structure
> that resulted from the monetary depreciations of the mid-
> sixteenth century forced Englishmen to abandon the old
> view of the 'commonweal' as a static condition. Thereaf-
> ter, the government was expected to play an active role in
> regulating the economy both to improve social conditions
> generally, and to prevent poverty wherever it could be at-
> tributed to identifiable economic causes.[126]

Theories such as these promoted the notion of state intervention in socio-economic matters, even to the point of joint action with private interests.

The later sixteenth century witnessed a shift in the European balance of economic power from Spain and the Mediterranean to North-West Europe, particularly to England, France and the Netherlands. English fishing activity in the Atlantic, not least on an axis from Ireland to Iceland and Greenland, had expanded appreciably from the late fifteenth century onwards. English activity in the Atlantic, however, expanded and changed greatly in the second half of the sixteenth century 'when national and London interests were drawn into it.' [127] This situation produced profound changes in England itself. Whereas 'in 1540 France was the place for a gentleman to win honour, in 1590 [it was] the Atlantic.' The fact that landed fortunes were unstable in this period, and that younger sons were especially plentiful for a couple of generations, gave added strength to the movement. This situation affected the thinking of men such as Sir Thomas Smith (1513-77), 'a leading political and intellectual figure' who 'in the early 1570s embarked on a colonial scheme in eastern Ulster' which 'had a double purpose: the enrichment of himself and his son, and the simultaneous strengthening of England's position in Ireland.' [128] Smith appealed to socio-economic criteria in order to justify his proposal regarding colonisation. Thus 'Smith's colonial ideas can be related to his more general political theory about the orientation of economic ambitions and social forces towards the public good'.[129] Smith contended that England was overpopulated. He argued that 'the dissolution of the monasteries had doubled the number of gentlemen and marriages. Smith had considered the neighbouring countries and found them well populated. However, "Ireland is the Queen's inheritance, many countries there, as that which I demand, given to her by act of Parliament of the same realm; others hers by dissent, the which lie almost desolate".' [130] Regarding Smith's argument concerning the overpopulation of England, he

> was concerned about what he believed to be the most dynamic section of English society - the younger sons of the gentry. Not only had the dissolution of the monasteries increased the population, it had also left the younger sons without livelihood or abode. Furthermore, they were impeded by primogeniture and inflation. His enterprise was thus 'a fit match for younger brothers such as have annuities, stipends and dead stocks to live on'.

Smith 'was justifying his enterprise by presenting it as a means of fulfilling the social needs of this class.' Moreover, 'the importance of the colonial territory in Smith's theory must also be recognized. In this the emphasis is put on the "waste", "desolate" and "vacant" land, which the indigenous population only thinly inhabits and inadequately exploits, so that the colony is presented as a venture in developing an underdeveloped area.' [131]

'London merchants who joined wholeheartedly in the privateering drive after 1585 followed this up, two decades later, by becoming backers of sustained colonisations. The support of their capital and experience was essential to both. Their interest dates back to the weakening of Antwerp's trading pre-eminence after midcentury and the signs of saturation in England's old continental markets, which led them to look further afield for trading opportunities.' [132] There was a very close connection between trade, industry, colonisation and the exploitation of the indigenous resources of the region settled.[133] Moreover, at that stage of economic development, investment in land or in the national debt constituted the only real outlets for the surplus profits of trade.[134]

By the 1580s the policy of plantation was well underway in Ireland. That programme of colonisation both reflected and further promoted political, social and economic trends in England. The Plantation of Munster, which followed the overthrow of the earl of Desmond in 1583, was promoted by the English government as a joint enterprise between the crown and private interests. Accordingly, this marked an important stage in the development of England as a mercantilist state and an important point of departure in socio-economic development. Thus the 'colonizing work was put in the hands of private projectors seeking to make profit from it, and its scale greatly expanded.' [135] Thus the Munster Plantation formed the model for the 'application of the joint-stock principle to colonisation',[136] a principle which was to be developed even more in connection with the later plantations in North America.

The successful undertakers engaged in the plantation have been described as 'men who had wealth and influence in England, but who required pioneering qualities too, resourcefulness, physical courage, ruthlessness, business capacity, tenacity and conviction of their superiority to the Irish as well.' [137] The major undertakers, many of whom were younger sons of English landowners and debarred from inheritance by the increasingly common practice of entailing estates, were attracted by the prospect of power and land.[138] Not surprisingly, these men tended to pursue their own interests rather than those of the government [139] and were animated more by greed than any notion of raising the Irish to civility.[140]

By the early seventeenth century, as a consequence of English military victory and subsequent colonisation, Ireland had become a colony dominated politically and commercially by its sister kingdom, England. Even Irish commercial interests had been made subservient to the interests of the developing English mercantilist state. Thus

> the Irish economy [in the seventeenth century] was conditioned by the connection with England in two distinct ways: economic activity was directly affected by government policies in Ireland, and the use of Irish resources was indirectly limited and confined by government policies formulated for England without regard to their effects upon Ireland. The results were not always disadvantageous: conflicts of interest between the two economies were present, but they were restricted by the fact that in some important respects England and Ireland complemented rather than competed with one another.[141]

Thus the first half of the seventeenth century saw significant economic growth, development and change. 'From a woodland society Ireland was emerging as an agricultural region with a substantial agricultural surplus.' [142]

The political consequences of the conquest, however, were far from advantageous for the native Irish, who remained the majority population on the island, for in Ireland 'a ruling class had been created, riddled with cultural, religious and economic differences, but united against Catholicism and Gaelic tradition.' [143] †

---

† This essay is based on a paper given to the Desmond Greaves Summer School in 1994.

2. THE GAELIC RESPONSE TO CONQUEST *

BREANDÁN Ó BUACHALLA

The study of early modern Ireland has been particularly productive in recent years. And although it could be said that it has produced its own variety of *odium theologicum*, a substantial body of original research has been produced which not only provides new data and novel insights but which also establishes the parameters for future study. One significant aspect of the burgeoning historiography is the utilisation by several scholars [1] of Irish literature as an essential tool in interpreting the period and in understanding the *mentalité* of the native intelligentsia. The fact that their research has not yet been incorporated into the received canon does not diminish its importance as a corrective and an indispensable alternative perspective to the monolingual one still in vogue. [2] The book under review is the most recent contribution to the field and the most ambitious so far. [3]

Dr O Riordan's approach differs from that of previous scholars in that she does not attempt a comprehensive survey of the period or of its literature but rather a specific thematic study set in a chronological framework. Certain themes which the author perceives as being crucial to an under-standing of bardic poetry and of the Gaelic aristocratic mentality - 'Unity, Sovereignty and Acceptance of the *Fait Accompli*' (p 21) - are examined, described, illustrated and interpreted and their manifestation in the poetry traced from the thirteenth to the seventeenth centuries. However the progression is not absolutely chronological, for although the

---

* This essay is based on a review of *The Gaelic Mind etc*, by M O Riordan, see endnotes on p 94.

first chapter deals primarily with the thirteenth century and the last chapter with the seventeenth, poems from different centuries are discussed in all chapters according as the subject matter demands. The emphasis throughout is on the similarity of the material - irrespective of date - and on the total correlation between bardic text and aristocratic mentality:

> The fundamental perceptions of the Gaelic world which were given a literary form in the bardic poetry were those also governing the activities of the Gaelic political world under the leadership of the Gaelic political elites (p 6).
>
> Likewise, the stability of the fragile structure carefully maintained by the poets is perhaps a reflection of a similar fragility in the political and social structures of early modern Ireland (p 17).
>
> The opening chapter thus deals first in a general way with some of the different themes which occur in the earliest and latest bardic poetry. This is done primarily to introduce the tone of the poetry and to indicate the similarity of the earlier material to the later (p 19).
>
> In the epilogue which follows the final chapter, an attempt has been made to follow the chosen themes through to the mid- and in some instances, the late seventeenth century, in order to illustrate the longevity of the themes and motifs of the bardic idiom ... (p 20).
>
> The poets' articulation of events of very different periods between the thirteenth and seventeenth centuries in the same idiom suggests that ... the themes and motifs were not simple literary devices, but represented the literary dilution of fundamental perceptions of the Gaelic aristocratic world (p 35).

Although previous scholars have differed in their approach to the literary material and, particularly, in their conclusions, they do share a common understanding: that the literary texts of the period manifest evidence of change, new perceptions, a new awareness among the literati and that these are to be interpreted as a reflex of contemporary social, cultural and political upheaval. Those scholars' efforts are unsatisfactory, the author claims, and the material has been misinterpreted, because of the neglect of two factors:

> First, it must be borne in mind that the bardic poetry is the work of professionally trained poets, a literary caste evolved over centuries writing in a genre which is in no way concerned with presenting a chronological account of Gaelic Irish experiences, but which nevertheless of its nature reveals aspects of the nature of Gaelic perceptions. Because of the literary nature of the poets' works, an element of artistic creativity is inevitable in the poetry, preventing any simplistic evaluation of the material. Second, the bardic material is particularly susceptible to the distorting influences of post-colonial historiography. The nationalism of the nineteenth and twentieth centuries in conjunction with the philosophy of many Gaelic revivalists has given rise to an excessively simplified interpretation of bardic motif and mentality. ... Many who succeed in avoiding the trap outlined above, however, produce interpretations of bardic poetry, which, while they may not be dominated by an overriding need to provide anachronistically ancient roots for nineteenth century Irish nationalism, are nonetheless dominated by an awareness of 'the Conquest' (pp 7-8).

It is argued that the similarity of the bardic material, from the thirteenth century to the seventeenth, 'is a testament to the continual and universal significance of the perceptions articulated by the poets' (p 8) and, accordingly, that bardic poetry is to be examined as 'a cypher of the Gaelic Irish aristocratic mentality' (p 17) in order to provide 'a referential basis from which to approach the hectic sixteenth and seventeenth centuries' (p 17). Neither that mentality nor the referential basis of the poetry changed over time and to suggest that they did - particularly in response to 'conquest' - is to impose an 'anachronistic interpretation' on the poets' 'intentions and perceptions' (p 20). An alternative frame of reference is proposed by the author, one which attempts to understand the poets' works 'in their own terms of reference' (p 20) and thereby 'to return their voice to those who articulated the mores of Gaelic society for over four centuries' (p 20). In contrast to other scholars, the author posits a framework which precludes the possibility of innovation, novel perceptions or any new awareness in the poetry and she insists that though indeed the socio-cultural context changed over time the poetry did not - and could not - reflect that change. Put at its simplest, the thesis being advanced is:

> To coincide with the enormous political and social changes which occurred during the sixteenth and seventeenth centuries, one might expect parallel changes in the poets' works. ... Changes in the poetry corresponding directly to political and social changes initiated by the centralised government, do not occur (p 5).
> The fundamental concepts of power ... remained fundamentally unaltered in the Gaelic Irish aristocratic mentality, to the end of the seventeenth century (p 6).

Since the author's thesis is in fact an antithesis, a reaction to what she perceives as exaggerated and unwarranted claims for change and innovation by other scholars, her approach is unidimensional in that it concentrates on one criterion - continuity - and ignores all others.[4] Of course, the author is right to stress the traditional nature of the poets' materials; that they had access to a range of derived modes, motifs, themes and conceits on which they could draw as the occasion demanded (the same applied to English, Welsh and French poets, of course); that the technical apparatus available to them - precedent, analogue, apologue, topic - by which they articulated their perceptions and plied their trade was employed by them in the seventeenth century as in the thirteenth. No scholar, I imagine, would question the fact that poets in the seventeenth century could still manipulate the traditional material or that much of the thematic inventory of seventeenth-century poetry was derivative. Indeed, that understanding would be part of the received wisdom. But it is not the point, nor the question at issue. Thus when the author states that:

> Much of the bardic poetry of the thirteenth and fourteenth centuries does not appear to be appreciably different in style or content to the bardic poetry of the early seventeenth century for instance (p 23).

one could hardly demur at the general premise, although one would expect some discussion of the implications of the qualifiers *much, appear* and *appreciably* and some consideration of the extent to which the poetry of those centuries is different - appreciably or otherwise. Similarly, when the author states that 'the poets' idiom remained basically very much the same throughout the period' (p 37), one would like some elaboration since it is implicit in the modified premise that some change did indeed take place. But those questions are not addressed. And when the author points out that the 'early Tudor period' was one 'when the foundations of the Gaelic world were coming under increasing pressure', but that this 'is not evident in the poems presented here' (p 21), one cannot but ask what of the poems not presented here? The fundamental question raised by the author's approach appertains to the referential framework employed by her: does a framework of continuity adequately cover the data? Is that the paradigm which emerges from the source material? I doubt it. In seeking and seeing only continuity, the author has in fact replicated the mistake of some of the work she severely criticises, work which sees only change - terminal decay - in the same material.[5] Continuity and change are not mutually exclusive criteria. In fact, change within continuity has been the central pattern of the Irish cultural tradition and it is the functional paradigm which can most meaningfully be applied to seventeenth-century Irish poetry.

The author's thesis is not consonant, it seems to me, with the available evidence and it is, accordingly, untenable. It is, however, a challenging and novel thesis which warrants a comprehensive and informed critique.

I

The main weaknesses of the book, particularly of the earlier chapters, originate primarily in the partial character of the data presented, the methodology employed in assessing it and the narrow - indeed myopic - nature of the focus. The author's claim that the 'multiplicity of bardic themes ... provide the major part of contemporary Gaelic records for the sixteenth and seventeenth centuries' (p 8) is manifestly inaccurate. Bardic poetry is undoubtedly the premier medium of extant writing in Irish for the sixteenth century but by the seventeenth that was no longer so. The variety of the sources available - both in prose and verse - make the seventeenth century one of the most diverse and prolific eras in the history of Irish literature and it provides an unprecedented richness of source material for the historian. Unfortunately most of those sources are not considered in this book as the author confines herself to a very narrow segment of the available material. Prose, for the most part, is ignored. I must admit that I fail to see how any scholar could undertake a study of either the Gaelic 'mind' or 'world' in the seventeenth century and ignore such primary texts as

Keating's *Foras Feasa ar Éirinn*, O'Sullivan Beare's *Historia Catholicae Iberniae Compendium*, the anonymous *Pairlement Chloinne Tomáis* or O'Flaherty's *Ogygia*. That criticism may be deemed unfair insofar as the author does make it clear in the introduction that her source is bardic poetry, but even accepting that parameter, one must still question the basis on which certain poems were selected for inclusion and others excluded from the study.[6] The bardic poems chosen and presented in the first chapter to illustrate the themes of 'unity' and 'sovereignty' are undoubtedly representative of the relevant genres and they do provide helpful insights into the bardic idiom and its socio-cultural matrix. But even in the first chapter - given the representative nature of the texts - fundamental objections can be raised concerning the methodology and the conclusions arrived at. The primary strategy employed by the author in the elaboration of her thesis is to quote and compare *some* verses from poems of different eras to demonstrate their similarity in theme, treatment and import. In no instance is any entire poem quoted or compared *in toto* to another. For the most part, the reader is therefore dependent on the author's analysis and interpretation of the poems under discussion. The very first instance of the application of this strategy clearly manifests its inherent methodological weakness. Three poems - from the fourteenth, sixteenth and seventeenth centuries respectively - are presented, analysed, summarised, quoted from and compared thus:

> A poem attributed to Tadhg Camchosach Ó Dálaigh, a poet of the later fourteenth century. calls on Niall Óg O'Neill, a northern chieftain of the Uí Néill, to unite Ireland and to rescue Banbha: *Sí ag Éirionnchaibh dá éis soin …*

Having been the property of foreigners for a time, she now belongs to the Irish. The partner with whom Art mated was in trouble and has been rescued.

Inis Fáil's being held by a foreign army; lust for the possession of Banbha with the fair rich grass; pillaging in every part of Ireland - these have been the cause of Ireland's woe.

No woman was ever in a plight like that of Inis Fáil (the land to whose aid St Patrick came) until she was rescued by the king of sweet mute Clan Breagh.

(Niall) departs not by (even) a (single) step from the advice of Aodh to his heir. He will unite together every plain and field, by his exploits. He will merit the efficacy of the blessing.

It is Niall, son of Aodh, high-king of all, who is (referred to) in Bearchán's prophecy. It cannot be gainsaid that he, whom Aoibheall prophesied, will be victorious.

Ó Dálaigh describes Ireland as being overrun by foreigners, this fact coupled with the pillaging of internal and external rivals and enemies of Ireland has caused Ireland's downfall. Niall O'Neill, son of Aodh, however, has 'united' Ireland and espoused her. His validation is his actual power and the fact also that he is the 'prophesied' one.

Some two hundred years later (*c* 1590s) Mathgamhain Ó hUiginn wrote the following stanzas for the *duanaire* of Feidhlim mac Fiachaidh O'Byme, chief of the Uí Bhroin of Gabháil Raghnall: *Níor saoileadh go teacht asteagh* ... :

An encampment of foreigners against the field of the Gael was not expected, a host who delayed in fighting - until they overwhelmed the Irish, (in spite of Feidhlim).

He was not sparing of his blood in battles, he did not turn from danger interweaving spears, creating havoc

until he excited the venom of the foreigners. The ser-
pents are the foreigners of Gort Breagh, the lions
(are) the warriors of Leinster. He has revived us.
Feidhlim is the prince of the lions.
The Leinstermen yield not to the destruction of the
foreigners, they do not take up arms (in vain?) - from
the day that the O'Byrnes are prepared their rapacity
destroys themselves.

Once again, 'foreigners' have overtaken Ireland and destroyed Banbha. However, the arrival of Feidhlim has
curtailed their activities. He like Niall has resisted the foreigners. Like the enemies of Niall also Feidhlim's enemies
have undone themselves by their greediness regarding the
land of Banbha. Feidhlim O'Byrne's prowess as a warrior
has destroyed their advance. As in the case following
O'Neill's victory, Ireland is saved, she is similarly saved
on the occasion of Feidhlim's victories from a fate similar
to that faced by her two centuries earlier in Niall O'Neill's
time.

Fear Flatha Ó Gnímh's poem of the seventeenth century following the departure of O'Neill, O'Donnell and
sundry other northern chiefs, in September 1607, re-
echoes the sentiments of both preceding poems in its perceptions of Ireland's condition in the absence of a leader.
Before Niall O'Neill's emergence into power Ireland was
overrun by foreigners, likewise before Feidhlim O'Byme
proved his military strength, Ireland was also 'under severe pressure from foreigners'. Now, in Ó Gnímh's case,
the absence of the northern chiefs places Ireland in a
similar condition of distress ... (pp 23-26).

The author then quotes *three* (out of twenty-four) verses
from the third poem to illustrate the comparison:

They can be compared to the remnants of a slaughter
after their destruction, suffering in the gore of their

wounds or (they can be compared to) a returning fu-
neral party.
The glory of the Gael is extinguished by a cloud of
sorrow which covers them, as a rain-cloud obliterates
the sun; so anxiety overwhelms them.
A herd of foreigners in their cattle meadows, lime
towers in the place of their buildings - stacks on their
assembly mounds, their markets in every quarter.

The evident survival of the perceptions articulated in both
earliest and latest poems is quite remarkable considering
the tremendous changes and development which had
taken place in the intervening centuries ... (p 26).

I, for one, fail to see the similarity of sentiment or condition. The first two poems are traditional eulogies to local
lords; the third an elegiac exposé of Ireland's condition,
bereft not of any one particular leader, but of her nobility in
general. The specific circumstances of Ireland's condition in
the third poem differ considerably from the generalised
rhetorical description of her condition in the other two and
the poem contains several novel sentiments and themes
which are totally lacking in the earlier poems, some of which
are, in fact, unprecedented in Irish political poetry. The
following notions seem to me to be of particular significance:

1. The Irish are now like captives under a foreign
    force;
2. Foreign kine have ploughed up the greens of Ireland;
3. Ireland (because of her physical and socio-cultural
    metamorphosis) will become another England;
4. The Irish are now deemed to be foreigners in Ire-
    land;
5. The plight of the Irish nobles fleeing from Ireland is
    to be compared to that of the children of Israel;

6. It is a pity that a second Moses has not rescued the
   Irish from their bondage;
7. If Providence ordains that Ireland is to become a
   New England *(Saxa nua)* then it were better to for-
   sake her.[7]

Those sentiments (and others) give the poem a tone and
configuration which set it apart from the earlier poems and
they have bestowed on it a significance not accorded to
them. But it is this very significance which is denied by the
author: the poet is merely utilising derived themes, conceits
and motifs and the poem is to be read *solely* in relation to its
supposed literary precedents and analogues, not as a literary
reflex of contemporaneous affairs. To prove her point, the
author cites this poem again when discussing another theme
and compares it to two other poems, the basis of comparison
being that 'in all three poems, Ireland is in distress, her poets
are sorrowful, a cloud of sorrow covers her' (p 53).

The first of the three poems being compared is a eulogy
on Maurice FitzMaurice, second earl of Desmond (d 1358)
in which the poet castigates the king of England for delaying
the honorand in England and depriving Ireland of his
presence. The author describes the poem and compares it to
the other poems thus:

> The poem begins on an apparently sharp note of displeas-
> ure with the monarch of England: *Mór ar bfearg riot a rí
> Saxan ...*
>
>> Great is our anger against thee, O king of England;
>> the ground thereof is that, though her spirit was high,
>> thou has brought sorrow upon Banbha.
>
> Before one goes on to place this stanza in its correct con-
> text, it is instructive to consider the longevity of this par-
> ticular bardic sentiment into a later period. Such an open-
> ing is easily transposable to the seventeenth century.

Compare, for instance, the sentiments expressed by Fear Flatha Ó Gnímh in the early seventeenth century: *Mo thruaighe mar táid Gaoidheal* [sic] ...

> Woe, the condition of the Gael, seldom now is any one of them in good spirits, their entire nobility are anxious.
> The glory of the Gael is extinguished by a cloud of sorrow which covers them, as a rain-cloud obliterates the sun; so does anxiety overwhelm them.

Ó Dálaigh in 1357 tells us:

> Because her lover is kept away from her, who had knit great fortune to her, the isle of Erin, the bright sunny one, is a sorrowful woman.
> The poets of the island of Fódla are sorrowful, and their fair ladies, since the young hero of Iomghán left Gabhrán's bright fortress.

Again in the seventeenth century Eoghan Rua mac a'Bhaird indicated the desolation of Banbha after the departure of O'Neill and O'Donnell: *Mór tuirse Ulltach fá n-airc* ...

> Great the sorrow of Ulster in her difficulty since Ó Domhnaill has been banished, and not less in grief is the North because of Aodh of Eanach.
> No laughter at children's play: an end to music: Gaelic is silenced: sons of kings unhonoured: no mention of winefeast or Mass.

In all three poems, Ireland is in distress, her poets are sorrowful, a cloud of sorrow covers her ... (pp 52-3).

That conclusion, is of course, true - in so far as it goes - but it conceals more than it elucidates and it attenuates rather than enriches our understanding of the poems. The 'similarity of the sentiments expressed in the extracts' (pp 53-4) is not obvious to me, I must admit, nor is the validity of the author's claim that 'The cause of Banbha's distress is attributed to the same source in each instance; the departure of the legitimate ruler/spouse' (p 55). That simplification not only obscures the major differences between the first poem and the other two but it ignores the quite different manifestations of Ireland's 'distress' depicted in them. In the poem on FitzMaurice, the honorand's temporary absence from Ireland is the sole cause of her distress; as a consequence, a general sorrow has descended on Ireland, her poets and nobles. In the other poems the manifestations of Ireland's distress are numerous, varied, specific, identifiable, and they appertain to disparate facets of Ireland's physical geography and her ethnocentricity: her fields, her woods; her music, language, religion. The author does point out that she is not claiming 'that the consequences of each departure were the same or even perceived to be similar by the poets' (p 55) but rather that 'This cannot be divined from the poets' use of the theme of Banbha's distress' (p 55). Assuming, for the sake of argument, that the three poems in question are in fact based on the same theme ('Banbha's distress'), it is obvious even from the few verses quoted by the author that the consequences of this distress were totally different for the poet of the early poem and for the poets of the later poems and that this difference is evident in the texts.

It is the presence of such new sentiments and themes in those and similar poems that have led other scholars to bestow significance on them and to utilise them as manifestations of change and of a new awareness among the literati. Contrary to the general consensus, the author holds that those poems are no different to bardic poems of previous centuries, that they merely continue into the seventeenth century derived themes and attitudes and that it is in the general context of bardic patronage that those poems must be considered:

Set in the centuries-old context of Gaelic consciousness in the bardic poetry ... the perceptions articulated by the latest and final phase of bardic endeavour are spared the contorting straitjacket of retrospective expectations. Rather than prefacing the poetry of the early 1600s with suggestions of a new awareness ... one might more profitably look backwards ... and recognise the intriguing continuity of perception surviving into the new century (p 122).

As a case in point the author takes another poem by Fear Flatha Ó Gnímh, 'Beannacht ar anmain Éireann' written apparently sometime after the flight of the Earls in 1607. The opening verses set the tone of the whole - a desolate jeremiad on Ireland's forlorn condition:

A blessing upon the soul of Ireland, island of the faltering steps; methinks Brian's Home [a bardic name for Ireland] of the soft voices is pregnant with sorrow. The same as the death of Fódla is the suppression of her right and her faith, the degradation of her free sons and her scholars, if lays or letters are true.

It were hard for Banbha not to die after that gallant company of champions who went journeying to Spain - alas for the princes of Ulster!

Fear of the foreign law does not permit me to tell her sore plight; this smooth land of royal Niall is being washed with innocent blood.

In her is no love of feast-days, no, nor no recourse to the clergy: the mirth of her bardic companies is no more, the modesty of her maids is no more ... (IBP 26 §§ 1-5).

The author analyses and interprets the poem thus:

Ó Gnímh's own sense of politics is evident in this poem, his patrons are fled, their replacements have not yet come forward, his lamentations on their departure are a profes-

sional duty and a cultural necessity, perhaps also an expression of personal grief ... The flight of the earls undoubtedly had an enormous impact on events in Ulster ...
One must, however, look at Ó Gnímh's poem in assumed
ignorance of the ultimate consequences of such a flight.
The most important element in the flight for the poet is the
unexplained departure of his patrons. The loss of their
company and perhaps more importantly, their patronage
has bewildered the poet (pp 123-4).

I find it very difficult to relate that interpretation to the poem
in question or to locate anywhere in the poem textual
evidence to sustain it. In the course of the poem, the poet
bemoans the departure not only of Ulster nobles (O'Neills,
O'Donnells, Maguire) but the demise of the Irish nobility in
general - McCarthys, O'Sullivans, FitzGeralds, Moores,
O'Connors, O'Rourkes, etc. Their depleted state is tant-
amount to the death of Ireland; it is, in fact, doubtful if she
will ever recover. The fact that the poet perceives Ireland's
woe in an all-Ireland perspective and not in a provincial
Ulster one is in itself interesting as is his claim that fear of
'the foreign law' prevents him from elaborating on Ireland's
plight. Nowhere in the poem does the poet allude to patrons
(either in specific or general terms) or to patronage nor are
any of the typical conceits of patronising verse invoked; he
addresses no particular lord or sept: it is public - as opposed
to personal - verse. Yet the author insists on locating the
poem within the framework of bardic patronage, of honorific
verse for patrons:

The death of Ireland is imminent because of the loss of
her chiefs. Principal among them are of course Ó Gnímh's
own patrons (p 124).
Considering, therefore, how affected the poets professed
to be by the death of patrons ... poems like those of Ó
Gnímh ... should not be a cause of surprise in their inten-

sity of feeling at the loss of very substantial patronage. It is against a background of the poet's relations with their patrons that such poems must be considered; whether the relation was actual or theoretical, the expression of it in the bardic poetry cannot be interpreted as figurative in one period and literal in another. Ó Gnímh therefore declares that Ireland is dead in the wake of the earls' departure ... (p 128).

From what we know of Ó Gnímh and his poetry, he never wanted for patronage and his main patrons throughout his life were the O'Neills of Clandeboy,[8] a sept not mentioned at all by him in this poem. The cause of Ireland's impending death is not 'the earls' departure' but the demise of the indigenous aristocracy of Munster, Leinster, Connacht and Ulster; but that is not the only manifestation of Ireland's impending doom; the poet also decries:

> The suppression of her right and faith, the degrada-
> tion of her free sons ... Fear of the foreign law does
> not permit me to tell her sore plight; this smooth land
> ... is being washed with innocent blood ... (IBP 26
> §§2-4).

The tone of the poem as a whole and the specific allusions to 'right', 'faith', 'foreign law', 'innocent blood' set it apart from the traditional bardic personal elegy, yet it is with two such typical elegies that this poem is further compared; to poems bemoaning the 'loss to Ireland' of Thomas Mag-auran's death in 1343, the 'misfortune' of Ireland on the death of Ulick Burke, chief of Clann Rickard, in 1424 (pp 129-131). No distinction is made between the death of an individual patron and the death of Ireland, nor between the derived attendant hyperbole of the funereal elegy and the new catacylsmic manifestations (albeit also hyperbolic) of an unprecedented crisis. The author instead stresses 'the persistence of traditional perspectives' (p 134) in the poems and she alerts the rest of us to 'the inadvisability of seeking new perceptions in the poetry' (p 140). It is this attitude - one suggestive of a lack of openness to the texts - which precludes the author from looking at the totality of the evidence, from examining the poem in question *in toto*. Accordingly, only five verses (out of seventeen) are quoted (pp 125-30) to elucidate this particular poem - those in which specific mention is made of the Ulster nobility (O'Donnells, O'Neills, Maguire) and of O'Rourke. The verses in which the poet laments the demise of various Leinster, Munster and Connacht septs and the crucial verses (quoted above) in which reference is made to 'right', 'faith', 'innocent blood', etc are not alluded to but are significantly ignored: a curious method of allowing 'the poetry to speak for itself' (p x), the author's avowed aim.

The author's treatment of those two poems by Ó Gnímh is especially illuminating in that it reveals her general approach to the material and identifies its central inadequacy. Her unidimensional focus - one which seeks and identifies only received conceits, perceptions, themes - apparently precludes her from the possibility of finding change in conjunction with continuity or of the admissability of new perceptions being mediated through traditional modes:

> The antiquity of the themes thus addressed highlights the vanity of seeking to tie the poetry too closely to the passing contemporary events (p 96).

Her determined - even deterministic - pursuit of the thesis induces a tunnel-vision which sees only that which supports the thesis and hides from purview any alternative evidence.

II

One obvious example of a 'new perception' among the literati, one which is articulated unambiguously in the poetry of the period, is their awareness of the presence in Ireland of people of a different religion to the Irish. Parallel to that awareness is their perception - a totally new one - that the war in Ireland is now a religious conflict, one being fought, as one poet put it, between 'General Patrick' on one side and 'Captains Luther and Calvin' on the other.[9] I should add that this new perception is not found in *all* the poetry of the period nor in the works of *all* poets; it is nevertheless prevalent and its emergence and development from being a new perception to being part of an orthodoxy can be traced *in the poetry* from *c* 1550 to 1650. Its textual presence is, however, ignored by the author as is its impact on related themes. One such theme - the banishing of foreigners from Ireland - is introduced thus by the author:

> This theme of banishing foreigners, so often encountered, is of major importance. It appears regularly in the poetry from the thirteenth to the seventeenth centuries. It is a bardic theme most open to misinterpretation in the light of later Irish nationalist historiography (p 41).

It would also seem to be open to misinterpretation by other versions of Irish historiography.

In keeping with the author's aim of demonstrating the continuity and unchanging nature of derived themes over time, it is here implied that this theme is essentially the same in the thirteenth and seventeenth centuries. In fact, it underwent a significant mutation in that the foreigners being banished in the seventeenth century were not the same as those being likewise threatened in previous centuries. Throughout the medieval period, 'foreigners' *(Gaill)* denote the Anglo-Normans: in the seventeenth century, they denote only the New English. In the interim the literati have accepted the Old-English as fellow Irish Catholics and the common denomination of *Éireannaigh* is applied to them and to the native Irish. Moreover, the prophetic texts, which throughout the middle ages foretold the eventual banishment of the 'foreigners' *(Gaill)* from Ireland, by the seventeenth century prophesied the expulsion of 'Sasanaigh' (the English), of 'heretics', of 'followers of Luther and Calvin'; and only those are now deemed to be foreigners in Ireland. It is a major shift - in perception, awareness and semantics - but one which is ignored by the author. Also ignored is a similar mutation in the theme of unity. As the author points out, a commonplace in bardic poetry is the poets' exhortation to unity among the Irish, one of the themes which survived into the seventeenth century (and even later). What is not pointed out is that the unity being called for in the seventeenth century is unity between the native Irish and the Old-English (under the common name of *Éireannach*) in a common thrust against the New English. Those thematic mutations provide a revealing insight into the skilful manipulation of old themes for new purposes by the literati. A crucial component of their survival-kit - and one which served them well from the coming of Christianity down to the nineteenth century - was their expertise in filtering new wine into old bottles. Since the author confines herself only to an examination of the bottles, the complexity, sophistication and changing texture of the contents elude her.

For instance, the theme and concept of sovereignty are discussed throughout the book and its traditional ideology explained and portrayed in different poems from the thirteenth to the seventeenth centuries. Implicit in the author's treatment of the theme is the unchanging nature of the concept and of its realisation in Irish poetry. But change it did - however imperceptibly - as is evidenced by the emergence of the metonymic use of *an choróin* ('the crown'), the application of the term *rí coróna/rí corónta* ('crowned king') to denote legitimate kingship'[10] and the acceptance by the literati of the concept of primogeniture as a concomitant of their allegiance to the Stuarts.

The complex of new perceptions that I have alluded to above - an awareness of major changes in the socio-cultural and politico-religious spheres of Irish life, changes appertaining in particular to language, religion and ethnicity - constitutes, it seems to me, a major difficulty for the thesis being advanced by the author. The evidence for such new perceptions is abundant in the literature of the period (in both prose and verse; in Irish, Latin and English sources) but even within the narrow restricted stratum of material examined by the author, similar evidence can equally be delineated. The following poems, it seems, are at least suggestive of change in the perceptions of the literati:

1. *Fúbún fúibh a shluagh Gaoidheal*, ed B Ó Cuív, 'A Sixteenth-Century Political Poem', *Éigse*, 15 (1974), 261-76.
2. *Dia libh, a laochruidh Gaoidheal*, ed S Mac Airt, *Leabhar Branach, The Book of the O'Byrnes* (Dublin, 1944), p 35.
3. *A Bhanbha, is truagh do chor*, ed DMM 28.
4. *Tairnig éigse fhuinn Ghaoidheal*, ed ND 1.
5. *Maith an sealad uair Éire*, ed DER 13.
6. *A leabhráin ainmnighthear d'Aodh*, ed DER 3.

I have chosen those texts - rather than several others - for it is in them that the new perceptions are initially and/or most eloquently enunciated; moreover, they have all been instanced by other scholars as evidence for some such change. They share one other feature in common: not one of them is quoted, let alone discussed, in this book. The author cannot have been unaware of the existence of these poems, nor of the claims made for them, and her decision to ignore them is indicative of a rather partial and unobjective attitude to the evidence. The first item in the above list is of some significance since it seems to be the earliest *poem* (it was written *c* 1541) in which an awareness of change is reflected in the literature.[11] The fact that the change relates to the cultural, political and religious spheres renders its importance all the more pivotal and its exclusion from the data presented in this book all the more questionable. Two of the poems in the list (5, 6) were written by (or are ascribed to) the same poet - Eoghan Rua Mac an Bhaird. The author does in fact deal with this poet and his poetry (pp 122-4, 184-202) but not with these specific poems of his - a curious omission. Similarly curious is the absence of any reference to or analysis of poem 2 above. This was one of the primary texts quoted by Dr Brendan Bradshaw as evidence for 'a new self-conscious nationalism ... a new national political consciousness and a nationalist ideology' in late sixteenth-century bardic poetry.[12] Dr Bradshaw and his thesis are roundly castigated by the author (pp 8, 73, 102) but the evidence he presented in support of his thesis is studiously ignored: an unusual and, I would maintain, unacceptable methodological stratagem. Another equally unacceptable stratagem employed by the author is to trenchantly criticise and refute theories/ideas not advanced by anyone. For instance, we are told that:

> Any suggestion that the works of these two poets contained the germinating seeds of nationalism or a concept of faith and fatherland, in the late sixteenth century, must be rendered meaningless when one considers the two poems above (p 90).

I am not aware that any scholar has claimed the existence of the concept of 'faith and fatherland' in any *sixteenth-century* poem nor the existence of 'the germinating seeds of nationalism' in the work of the poets in question.[13] The two poems mentioned by the author are traditional eulogies commemorating the martial careers of one of the chiefs of the O'Byrnes (Aodh mac Seáin d 1579) and of Thomas Butler, 10th Earl of Ormond (1534-1614) and the author's comment on them reveals an unsettling aspect of her general attitude to the material: her expectation of consistency in all things at all times by the poets. Because certain characteristics or perceptions have been posited for certain poems, they should be ever-present and all-pervasive, it seems:

> If one is to regard Hugh mac Shane O'Byme as a member of the "more patriotic Gaelic nobility", and see reflected in his *duanaire* the stirrings of an Irish nationalist consciousness and if this in turn can be said to indicate a burgeoning nationalist awareness among the poets as a body, then the poems addressed to an Old English lord of different loyalties and different religion should reflect some of this new political awareness ... (p 80).

The author's interpretation of the acceptance by the literati of the status quo is central to her reading of the poetry and to her thesis in general. Having studied the related themes of 'Unity, Sovereignty and Acceptance of the *Fait Accompli*' in the first chapter, the author concludes that the themes studied:

> are linked with the concept of the able suitor being the most worthy; the most successful military hero deserves the spoils of his victories. This, in turn, logically extends to the fundamental principle of might is right (p 60).

The basis for that conclusion is a study of several poems (from the thirteenth, fourteenth and fifteenth centuries) in which Norman lords are praised in traditional eulogistic terms by the poets and are treated no differently than native lords. The author notes:

> The alacrity with which the poets acquiesce in the *de facto* power of the addressee and in the *fait accompli* whether the victor be native or foreign ... Banbha is willing to be subdued by the strongest arm (p 60).

This conclusion is extended by the author from the medieval period to the sixteenth and seventeenth centuries and it forms a constant *leitmotif* of her general thesis.[14] The author's analysis, it seems to me, is a very simplistic extrapolation of a very complex (and changing) situation and I would question its validity in adequately describing and comprehending the ambivalent, volatile. shifting attitudes of the Gaelic lords to the ever-encroaching central power in the late-sixteenth century. Even when applied to earlier centuries, it still seems to be an inadequate model. Several obvious questions arise: was the attitude of the native intelligentsia uniformly the same to *all* Norman lords? [15] Did it undergo any shift or mutation from century to century or from province to province? Did the native intelligentsia distinguish between the 'Gaelicised' Norman lords and those - particularly in the Pale - who were not culturally assimilated? Was there any correlation between the acceptance by the poets of the *de facto* power of Norman lords and the same lords' willingness to cultivate Irish learning - and to subsidise its practitioners? Was the poets' attitude to Norman power/influence uniformly and always the same at local and at national level? Can any distinction be made between the poets' attitude to the temporal power in pre- and post-Reformation Ireland? Only the latter question is raised in this book - and answered with an emphatic *no*. According to the author, the attitude of the Irish literati to temporal power was the same in the sixteenth and seventeenth centuries as in the medieval period, an attitude informed solely by the principle 'of might is right' and predicated on the acceptance of the *fait accompli*. The author puts it more trenchantly:

> The most important conclusion to be drawn from this apparently dichotomous situation is that the possession of and successful maintenance of power or authority constituted the single strongest argument of right recognised by the poets, and thus by their supporters (p 49).
>
> The poets simply respected power; power which was visible or implied and which was competently wielded. The whole society revolved on this acceptance of the reality of the *fait accompli* (p 69).
>
> Acceptance of the *fait accompli* is perhaps the most enduring trait to emerge from the accumulative influences of the warlike society which was the world of both the poet and the chieftain ... (p 96).
>
> The willingness of the poets to acquiesce in the *fait accornpli*, and their praise of the strongest, is illustrative of their belief in the value of the obvious (p. 117).
>
> It is in their exposition of the fundamental precepts of unity, sovereignty and their tradition of acceptance of the *fait accompli* that the poets of the early seventeenth century manifest their adherence to the traditional values and perceptions enshrined in the literary medium and which remained valid for them and the majority of the Gaelic aristocracy until their decline at the end of the century (p 120).

If this is so, how does one explain the refusal of the poets - and their political leaders - to apply the all-pervasive principle of the *fait accompli* to either Cromwell or William III? Had the poets' attitude changed between the sixteenth and seventeenth centuries? Or did they apply other criteria, rather than that principle alone? Both, I believe: the poets' attitude to temporal power did undergo change between the sixteenth and seventeenth centuries and that attitude was far more complex than a unidimensional one of acceptance of the *fait accompli*.

The primary catalyst for the attitudinal change was the accession of James I to the crown of the three kingdoms in 1603, an accession accepted (on several grounds) by the ruling élites of Irish society and accordingly valorised by the intelligentsia. This did constitute an acceptance of the *de facto* power of the King, as King of Ireland, but it did not entail an acceptance of the socio-cultural changes as a *fait accompli*. Indeed part of the strategy of the Irish polity in coming to terms with James I was their hope and belief that he, by his grace and favour, would redress the legitimate complaints of Irish Catholics. The Irish literati could then simultaneously lament the passing of the old order and yet wilfully accept James I as their hereditary King; bemoan their own and their country's fallen fortunes and yet look forward to complete restoration; utilize the metaphor of the children of Israel as an analogue of both their desolate tale of woe and their predictions of ultimate victory. It is this crucial differentiation - in conception, semantics and application - between acceptance of the status quo or *de facto* power and refusal to submit to a *fait accompli* which is the key to an understanding of Irish Catholic political activity and its literary reflex in the early-seventeenth century. However contradictory or ambivalent the actions of the Irish nobility in 1641 may seem to us today - taking up arms in the name of the King - in the context of seventeenth-century politics it was both logical and coherent. The fact that neither the acceptance nor the valorisation of James was total or absolute - it applied only to his power *in temporalibus*, never *in spiritualibus* - is surely an indication of a well thought-out, sophisticated strategy, rather than the automatic application of a simple principle of acceptance of the *fait accompli*. That strategy is well reflected in the contemporaneous literature and two of the relevant texts (two poems of welcome to James I) are in fact discussed by the author (pp 169-76). They are not of any particular significance, however, the author claims; they do not reflect any novel attitude on the poets' part nor do they reflect political reality; rather are they to be interpreted in traditional terms and to be compared with earlier poems in which poets from different eras praised Norman lords; more specifically they are to be read in conjunction with a sixteenth-century poem in praise of Elizabeth I. As the author puts it:

> For James I was an illustrious and powerful king. His position as liege of their patrons exalted both them and the poet. Their evaluation of his worthiness was made ... according to the traditional bardic perception of the status of a powerful monarch... So also does their eulogising of James I assume a traditional tone ... (p 168).
> As king of Ireland, James is to be hailed, just as Elizabeth was by an earlier poet (p 172).

But Elizabeth I, in fact, was never hailed, by any Irish poet, as king (or sovereign) of Ireland; James was so hailed by the Irish intelligentsia in general. The poem on Elizabeth [16] is indeed fulsome in her praise, a panegyrical ode eulogising her virtues, her characteristics, both physical and mental, her martial exploits, her victories, her international status; but she is hailed only as *prionsa Sacsan* ('the sovereign of England'). James, on the other hand is hailed, accepted and legitimised as king *(rí)*, high-king *(ardrí)* and spouse *(céile)* of Ireland: a crucial and significant difference indicating a new departure on the part of the Irish intelligentsia and the Irish polity. And so was it understood by later seventeenth-century writers.[17] The author is, of course, right in pointing out that the Irish poets' eulogising of James assumes 'a traditional tone' (p 168). The literary modes, the themes, the metaphors are uniformly traditional; the message is not. James is not only valorised, by the traditional mechanisms, as king and as spouse of Ireland; he is also valorised as 'our king', and as a claimant to *coróin na hÉireann* ('the crown of Ireland'), one of the *trí coróna* ('three crowns'). Those concepts were unprecedented and hitherto unattested but they hereafter reverberate through Irish political poetry. The poems in question then are at once highly traditional and yet innovatory, a classic example of fundamental change being mediated through traditional modes.

But it is this very process, the poets' facility to present change in a traditional garb, their invocation and utilisation of tradition as an enabling mechanism in the acceptance of attitudinal, political and ideological change, that is lost on the author. Texts - all texts it seems - can be dissected into similar thematic parts; the presence of similar conceits or themes in different poems from different eras renders those poems similar in impact and significance, regardless of changing socio-political circumstances. Several simple questions suggest themselves: Is a traditional poem in the prophetic mode addressed to a minor chief with no political aspirations 'the same' as a similar poem addressed to O'Neill the night before the battle of the Yellow Ford? Is a fourteenth-century poem to a local lord in which he is hailed in traditional eulogistic terms as one fit (or prophesied) to be king of Ireland to be interpreted in identical terms as a similar poem addressed to James I, the *de facto* king of Ireland? Are all poems of similar theme and mode to be read in uniform fashion irrespective of addressee, context or milieu? Can changing circumstances change the impact or perception of a traditional poetic conceit? I believe so. To shift the focus of our investigation somewhat, Dryden's 'The Lady's Song' and Pope's 'Windsor Forest' are not obviously nor superficially Jacobite poems, but hackneyed derivative exercises in the pastoral mode. Read differently they are powerful contemporary political statements containing a seditious message which was clearly understood by a sympathetic clientele.[18] But such crucial considerations as decoding or contextualisation are not entertained by the author. Poems, it seems, are fixities of determinate signification: cultural artefacts built on discrete themes and motifs whose denotative potential is constant, whether written in the thirteenth, sixteenth or seventeenth centuries. As the author puts it:

> The poems ... studied in the earlier chapter, can be regarded as patterns for the use of motifs and themes which will re-appear in different historical contexts in the sixteenth century. While the historical context undoubtedly changed between the thirteenth and sixteenth centuries, the use of the motifs and themes are used in the same way by the later poets, for the same reasons and to articulate the identical world view (p 63).
>
> The works of the professional Gaelic poets of the seventeenth century reveal very little that is new in terms of altered perceptions in areas already discussed with regard to sixteenth-century bardic poetry (p 120).
>
> The import of the changes occurring found no corresponding adaptation in the world view of the poetry though adaptation in language and rhetoric took place harmoniously and naturally (p 234).

Since the author insists on interpreting poems only as autonomous discourse not amenable to a textual considerations of milieu or audience, no attempt is made to relate 'the word' to 'its world' [19] - a necessary exercise when dealing with political poetry - and, accordingly, poems are not presented in their appropriate context. Notwithstanding the emphasis placed by the author on the pervasive and central part played by the *de facto* syndrome in the intelligentsia's world view, poets who reflect it in the early seventeenth century are rebuked (or so it seems) for so doing and bemused surprise is registered at the unqualified praise addressed by different poets to Cormac O'Hara, lord of Leighne (1584-1612); Thomas Butler, 10th Earl of Ormond and to James I:

> No sense of latent patriotism ... prevented O'Hara from accepting the foreign office of seneschalship. It did not interrupt the copious stream of bardic encomium to him (p 114).
>
> His elegy for Ormond, written in or later than 1614, displays no sensitivity to, or even awareness of, the wider implications of Ormond's identity as an arm of the ever strengthening central administration (p 150).
>
> He [James] is credited by Ó hEodhusa as having successfully banished the ills of Ireland too, without any qualification ... No suggestion of religion, land settlements, local independence or any other contemporary problem is specifically mentioned or even hinted at (p 172).

Why should it? Court eulogy presents ideals of perfection, not concrete characteristics; it portrays an idealised character not reality, the notion of 'warts and all' being incomprehensible to its practitioners.

The author's argument, though disarming in its naïvety, reflects a simplistic attitude which is patently inadequate to deal with the complexities of either life or literature in early modern Ireland. Accordingly, the shifting kaleidoscope of socio-cultural and politico-religious change in which life was lived in the period is never incorporated into the author's framework; the various stances available to the intelligentsia in dealing with an unprecedented era of momentous transition are never examined nor are their strategies for survival assessed.[20]

III

In the final chapter ('Old Themes in a "New Order" '), the author widens the scope of her study to include non-bardic poetry, the work of non-professional poets like Haicéad and Céitinn and, in particular, the series commonly called 'political poems' [21] written between 1640 and 1660. The period in question (1600-1660) was one of profound change, not only in the social and political spheres but in the literary world as well: new themes, new metres, new modes, new types of poets, new literary classes emerge: it was a period of intense literary activity involving renewal, re-organisation and creativity. Yet in spite of those manifest changes - social, political, literary - the perceptions of the poets and of their poetry remained unchanged, the author maintains:

> That is to say that the seventeenth century produced poets whose abiding preoccupations mirrored those of their predecessors though their social and political context was rapidly changing (p 216).
> The innovations in literary form lead us to expect innovation in perception ... The most remarkable characteristic of the more well-known works of the seventeenth century poetry ... is its adherence to the perceptions traditionally articulated in bardic poetry ... and to the social and political preoccupations we have come to associate with the poetry of the schools (pp 217-8).
> For all the innovation in the literary style of these poems, a closer examination reveals that on the level of perceptual changes and evidence of dramatic change in Gaelic political consciousness these poems prove to be as rooted in the bardic field of reference and social exclusivity as the contemporary syllabic compositions (p 240).

It is in the light of those claims that the data is then interpreted - or rather, misinterpreted as I would argue. For it is in this chapter more than any previous one that the author's obvious enthusiasm for her thesis, her unflagging determination to validate it, her vigour in demonstrating the wrong-headedness of other scholars that leads her - wilfully or otherwise - to distort, ignore or misinterpret the textual evidence. Since that is a serious and major indictment, I feel it incumbent on me to deal with it at length and in some detail. The following are typical examples which can be easily tested against the evidence. I translate the relevant passages as literally as possible:

1. In *Óm sceól ar ardmhagh Fáil*, Keating's intention is that of the traditional poet, seeking to present a picture of Ireland deprived of Keating's own provincial lords, the Fitz-Geralds of Desmond ... (p 232).

This is not so. The opening two lines set the tone and theme of the whole: the poet's loss of sleep because of woeful tidings reaching him concerning Ireland and his suffering at the plight of her own people *(dála a pobail dílis)*. In the ensuing verses, he bemoans the rise of foreigners of low origin in Ireland and the demise of Ireland's native sons; he mentions particularly the O'Neills, the O'Briens, the Munster gentry in general, and the FitzGeralds not only of Desmond but also of Leinster. How this poem can be described as a 'picture of Ireland deprived of Keating's own provincial lords, the FitzGeralds of Desmond' baffles me.

2. His elegy for the two Butlers ... adheres to the rationale of belonging, and to the traditional criteria of power and offers no new perceptions on what was a very new situation (p 234).

In fact, the poem [22] in question is a very sophisticated elaboration of an entirely new perception: that the crucial differentiation to be made now in Ireland was not one of ethnic origin but of religious allegiance. Accordingly

Keating distinguishes in the poem between the Old English *(Sean-Ghoill/Fionn-Ghoill)* and the New; the former sharing mutual ties of blood and religion with the Irish *(báidh cleamhnais is cuisleann gaoil/comhbáidh creidimh do aontaoibh)*, the two groups being thus accounted as belonging to the family of Banbha *(do chloinn Bhanbha)* for whom the New English have nothing but hate and envy. The apposite verses are indeed quoted by the author but their significance is explained away.

3.　There is no evidence for the development of anything like a coherent new political consciousness based on religion or race in Haicéad's poem (p 244).

The poem in question *(Múscail do mhisneach a Bhanbha)* opens with a prose preamble (ignored by the author) in which the poet explains the circumstances in which it was composed: 'After the selfish group, the "faction" had raised their heads and displayed their treachery and fratricide in making peace with heretics and cutting themselves off, by guile and violation of oaths, from the body Catholic *(as an gcorp Catoilice)* namely the Confederation i.e. the confederation of peace, help and union which the Irish *(na hÉireannaigh)* made amongst themselves under oath to make war in defense of the true faith in Ireland'.

That seems to me to be a very lucid exposition of a coherent view of contemporary Irish affairs, one which is mediated through a consciousness based on common race *(Éireannaigh)* and common religion *(Catoilice).* The author's claim that 'Haicéad's adoption of the nuncioist cause effectively provided him with a sept allegiance substitute ... and he adapted the corresponding poem-type to his immediate needs' (p 244) gives a totally false impression of the poem which is a working out in literary form of the excommunication by the Hierarchy of those who had accepted the peace terms of 1646. The metaphors used throughout are not those associated with praise poetry addressed to a particular leader of a particular sept but metaphors emanating from the notion of mother Banbha being defiled, abused, betrayed by some of her own children: the only traditional theme in the poem - but a highly apposite one - is the children of Israel and the referential framework is Ireland - *a oileáin Éireann* ('O island of Ireland').

4. The manner in which the author of *An Síogaí Rómhánach* dealt with the events of the 1640s indicates no development in Gaelic political perceptions from that indicated in formal bardic poetry (p 255).

Yet on the following page we are informed that the same poet in the same poem 'traces the origins of the destruction of Banbha to the reign of Henry VIII' (p 256). That insight constitutes a major innovative development in Irish politico-religious perceptions and it is one which pervades seventeenth-century Irish literature. Put in simple terms, by 1630 Henry VIII had become the *bête noire* of early modern Irish historiography.

5. The concern of the author principally with the Ulster chiefs ... also illustrates the survival of the regional and provincial bases of loyalty and interest (p 262).

Undoubtedly the hero and central character of this poem is Eoghan Rua Ó Néill whose fame and exploits - at home and abroad - are celebrated exuberantly and whose untimely and tragic death is mourned. It is revealing - in the light of the author's analysis - to list some of the places mentioned by the poet in recalling Ó Néill's military exploits:

> He brought succour by force to the province of Ulster, he overturned the foreigners ... he encircled Dublin, he scourged the same county and pleasant Anglo-Irish Meath, he banished heretics from Maryborough and he

> scattered everybody from Banagher, he shook Birr, Nenagh and from there to Thomond; Iniskeen ... Waterford ... Duncannon ... Wexford ... New Ross and Howth ... Kilkenny, Shannonside, Blackwater, Fore, Barrow ... By the Suir his band was industrious and from there back again to the Erne ... (FPP ii: 146-72).

But it is not only in the geographical distribution of Ó Néill's military career that the poet's vista is seen to be broader and more inclusive than 'regional or provincial' loyalties would dictate. In the opening sequence, the narrator asks God how was it that the Irish - who refused to adore idols - were suffering and that Ireland was laid low. He then recounts the woes of Ireland from the time of Henry VIII to the outbreak of war in 1641; the welcome afforded to Ó Néill is expressed in national terms:

> By Mac Duach that was cheerful news on every harbour of the harbours of Ireland being proclaimed, being mentioned, being prophesied, being read that Eoghan Rua on the shoulders of the Irish would vanquish the cream of the English ... (*ibid* 179-83).

It is as a national hero also that Ó Néill is lamented, and although he, if he had lived, would have vanquished Cromwell, all is not lost:

> *Och ochón* my bitter woe ... a third of their sickness is not clear to me, but the Irish being vanquished, put down and afflicted by plague, famine and war destroying them ... Yet, however I have not lost hope and I will not be without some courage. God is stronger than the English horde. There still survive of the Milesian race Aodh Buí (Ó Néill) ... Féilim (Ó Néill) ... Colonel Farrell ... Hugh O'Byrne ... The band who are not to be trifled with by anybody still survive: O'Rourkes, O'Reillys, Walshs ... [23] the progeny of O'Connor ... O'Kelly ... McCarthy ... the O'Briens ... the Kennedys ... O'Carroll ... O'Sullivan ... That group

will shortly converge and unite together and defeat the
foreigners in Singland ... foreigners will not survive in
Ireland ... (*ibid* 230-7, 265-96).

Although one could dismiss that prophetic morale-booster as
being derivative in nature and rhetorical in intent, one
cannot, it seems to me, in the light of the *textual* evidence
claim that the poet's concern is 'principally with the Ulster
chiefs'. In a simple head-count of the contemporaneous
personages mentioned in the poem, the Ulster chiefs constitute a very small minority.

6. The poem known as *Aiste Dháibhí Cúndún* ... is written
    by a poet for whom the Ulster contribution to the conflict
    and the Ulster warriors meant little. Its sphere of interest
    lies in Connacht and Leinster (p 262).

The poet's sphere of interest is in fact Ireland - all Ireland -
and from the opening lines to the last that referential
framework is explicitly enunciated:

> Sorrowful is this state in which Ireland has fallen, like a
> messy dung-yard being filled by villains ... let the territory
> of Ireland be as it is for some time until the mercy of the
> high son of dear God comes like a messy dung-yard being
> piled on villains (FPP iii: 1-2. 313-15).

The only specific references to Connacht in the poem occur
in lines 31 and 217 where the poet laments the transplanta-
tion to Connacht; the only specific references to Leinster
occur in lines 234-65 where he mentions certain battles
fought there in the 1640s; he also, in the same passage,
refers to specific battles fought in Munster and to the
massacre of Drogheda in 1650. The only contemporaneous
personages mentioned in the poem are Alastair Mac Colla
(237), Lord Taafe (240), Rinuccini (245), the Earl of
Glamorgan (247), Cromwell (259) and the Pope (282). No
contemporaneous Irish leaders are mentioned so that the

author's contention that 'the Ulster warriors meant little' to the poet is, like many others advanced in the book, an *argumentum ex silentio*. In fact, in a learned historical interlude in the poem (110-150), introduced most probably to impress his audience, the poet mentions several Ulster heroes.

7. Cúndún's aspirations for Banbha do not extend much further than that the two southern septs of O'Brien and McCarthy be reinstated (p 265) ... Cúndún's resolution for the woes of Banbha is the restoration of the McCarthys and the O'Briens, the replacement of his provincial leaders (p 268).

These misleading and fallacious statements are based on a total misreading of certain lines in the poem in question. Rather than dealing with the reinstatement of the poet's 'provincial leaders' as claimed, the poet beseeches God to bestow on a chief of the McCarthys or the O'Briens the capacity to deliver Banbha and her people:

I beseech you Mary to succour this land ... I beseech John the Baptist and all the apostles ... to pray to Christ for our deliverance from the bondage, torment, distress in which the Irish have been for some time. And if God would only bestow a chief of the Irish, of the strong McCarthys or the noble O'Briens who would undertake a slaughter, who would inflict a massacre in a wound-inflicting mighty battle and who would dispatch by force the villains ... *Yes, by God, I'd swag my beaver* (FPP iii: 289-303).

8. His [Cúndún's] desolation and distress focussed entirely on his own relationship with the polity of his native province ... Cúndún's expression of grief at the reduction of the Munster nobility ... focusses entirely ... on the individual loss and its consequences (pp 268-9).

There is, in fact, no mention in the poem of the 'polity of his native province', let alone any focussing on the poet's relationship with it; nor is there any mention of the 'reduction of the Munster nobility'. Like several of the poems in this series, the poet does express sentiments indicating personal grief:

> Och, alas! My worry forever! Och! my pity, I cannot sleep. My ears cannot hear from worry and my eyes are closed with tears ... My heart and senses are bereft of strength and my health and limbs are feeble ... (FPP iii: 38-46).

One could argue, perhaps, that this personal element is more conspicuous in this poem than in the others. Yet, even here, no matter how personal the voice or how anguished the cry, the grief emanates not from 'individual loss' but from communal deprivation and destruction which afflicted both high and low, laymen and cleric and which is manifest throughout Ireland:

> Sorrowful is the state in which Ireland has fallen ... the nobility laid low without the possibility of rising, her heroes a heap of bones, I pity her women assembled together ... (FPP iii: 1-5).
> The kingdoms are without a king or a noble prince, and the nobility are worried because of this attack and the populace are involved in war and strife and the poor sadly defending Ireland ... (*ibid* 21-24).
> And from the coming of Christ to the end of the world, there was not, is not, and will not be imposed on any people descended from Eve, the likes of the bondage which the land of Ireland has endured. Now I will tell a portion of her (their?) story although it is a suffering in excess of my own pain. Painful to me is the narration of the Church of Ireland as I see her in want of priests and clerics ... (*ibid* 180-87).

> There is no torment under the sun of plague, famine, war
> or destruction which has not come to this land of Ireland
> ... (*ibid* 231-33).
> Since the day Cromwell made a pathway through blood
> ... and wrought in Drogheda a wound-dealing slaughter
> on women, children, men and heroes and inflicted this ter-
> ror all over Ireland ... I will relate, if I can, a part of their
> woe ... (*ibid* 259-68).

9. Munster is the area upon which the poet focussed his
    attention and the plight of the nobility of that province,
    especially of the Old English is the subject of his lamenta-
    tions. In this poem the Ulster hero Eoghan Rua is merely
    mentioned once ... (p 272).

I fail to understand the significance of the last sentence in
the above quotation. If Eoghan Rua were mentioned thrice,
would that change the focus and orientation of the poem? It
is but another disingenuous attempt by the author to dilute
the national framework in which the poem is written and to
deny the inclusive non-provincial focus of the poet. As for
the area on which the poet focussed his attention and the
people whose plight he bemoans, let us listen to the poet
himself:

> My day of woe until I die and until I am buried alone...
> the destruction of this race which has come upon you,
> Ireland ... when I see rout and slaughter, the heads of your
> heroes being put on spikes and your children being dev-
> astated and treated like a rabble ... If I were dead the
> news would not be a loss ... compared to the treatment of
> the progeny of the nobles of Ireland ... and of all those of
> Irish-English blood [24] who were steadfast ... FitzGeralds,
> Butlers, Burkes, Plunketts, De Courceys. Condons, Pow-
> ers, Roches, Barrys, Walshs ... (FPP v: 1-32).
> All who were left of the stock of the Irish who were in in-
> heritance, office or wealth were sent to Connaught in
> haste or to North Thomond hurriedly and instead of their

lands they were promised a barren patch in north Con-
naught, in Thomond or in Breifne ... (*ibid* 145-50).
You were always called the island of saints until you for-
sook all your characteristics ... small wonder that you
have fallen Ireland, you exchanged piety for gluttony ...
fraud, deceit, to top your manners, gave to the English the
possession of your labours, brought upon you the on-
slaught of major disaster, which crushed the bones of your
body, which cut your ligaments, your vigour and your
sinews, which discharged your veins, your powers and
your wounds. You lost your head, your children, your
husband: namely propitious bountiful Charles, your earls,
your lords, your champions: and Eoghan Rua Ó Néill of
the battles, your husband ... (*ibid* 361-2,373-4, 395-404).

As in the other poems in this series, this poet's canvas is
commensurate with Ireland, his concern her people, his
focus their plight. The claim that Munster is the focus of the
poet's attention is not borne out by an examination of what
the poet actually wrote.

10. It is important therefore to emphasise that the poets'
articulation of concern for the church and their dismay at
its physical or metaphorical destruction is independent of
the immediate circumstances of the mid-seventeenth century ... (p 287).

In elaboration of this claim, the author points out that the
interest of seventeenth-century poets in focussing on
'denominationally religious matters ... paralleled that of the
poets four hundred years earlier' (p 287). To prove her point,
the author quotes a *quatrain* from a fourteenth-century poem
in which the poet 'is concerned for the hazards to unpro-
tected churches' and compares this with *five* lines from a
seventeenth-century poem (of a hundred and forty-five lines)
in which the poet 'described the state of the churches in the
aftermath of the decade of conflict' (p 288). Apart from the

difficulty of ascertaining or identifying 'denominationally religious matters' in thirteenth-century poetry - anywhere in Europe - the author fails to see the crucial difference between the religious concerns of the poets in both periods. The latter poets' concern is primarily with the state of 'the Church', the 'Church of God', the 'Church of Ireland', the destruction of individual church buildings being but one symptom of the general destruction:

> Painful to me is the state of the church of Ireland, as 1 see her in want of priests and clerics, every church is a widow for some time and her monasteries are being demolished every day ... (FPP iii: 186-94).
>
> Any buildings or jewels which would serve the glory of God, they destroy ... they broke down every holy fair monastery, they plunder belfries and towers, crosses and churches ... every, graveyard is a railed fold for sheep or as an enclosure for their calves. They enforce a law on us banishing the clergy, every religious order, friars and Jesuits ... (FPP v: 229-42).
>
> The expulsion of the people to whom Ireland yielded and the church of God being transformed ... (ND i 26: 103-4).
>
> Her nobles were banished abroad. To top the torment her churches are without altars, without the mass, without reverence, like horses' stables, nor without a stone of their stones standing. Putrid is this story ... (DMM 49: 14-18).

The focus, the concerns, the framework are totally different. The plundering of churches was a common feature of medieval Ireland, one which is well reflected in bardic poetry; the notion of an institutional church - the Church of Ireland *(eaglais Éireann)* - being systematically destroyed occurs nowhere in medieval Irish poetry, nor would one expect it. No one would claim that the excerpts quoted above or similar passages in other poems reflect *in all aspects* an actual historical situation or that they can be always interpreted as factual records of specific circumstances. Some of the details are obviously based on historical facts (the destruction of churches, the expulsion of the clergy, the sacking of Drogheda); others are general, vague, figurative and polemical. However, these poems were not written as factual historical chronicles but as public rhetoric for a specific community at a specific period. Like all rhetoric, it is time-bound and culture-bound: it is the public rhetoric of post-Reformation Catholic Ireland - the equivalent of the public sermon in seventeenth-century England. And although written and narrated by individuals, the poems are addressed to a community with whom the authors identify and of which they count themselves one:

> The pastors of the flock were banished from us, we are the scattered wounded flock ... (DMM 49:23-24).
> Our harp lost its tuning fork by which Ireland's sorrow might be played ... (*ibid* 85-86).
> Misery has overtaken us all - the poor, the rich, the weak, the strong; the lord... and the ploughman; laity and clergy are under the same hurt and everybody bears his cross ... (*ibid* 60-65).
> Only a spark of our religion remains ... we ourselves brought about all that has happened ... (FPP iv:448-56).

The emergence of a communal 'voice' [25] in Irish political poetry is, perhaps, the most significant change in its narrative modes in the early modern period, but no matter how rhetorical or figurative the voice or its discourse, the excerpts given above depicting the wholesale countrywide destruction of churches, the banishment of the Catholic clergy and the persecution of believers could not be related to, nor could they have any contextual relevance in, pre-Reformation Ireland. Rather than being 'independent of the immediate circumstances of the mid-seventeenth century', as claimed by the author, the poets' concern for the church is a literary reflex of contemporary circumstances. Moreover, and more importantly, the poets' distress at the state of their church is but one component of their overall concern for Ireland and the body politic. Such an innovative religious concern is not found in medieval Irish poetry and it constitutes a central part of the intellectual mutation which the Irish intelligentsia underwent between the sixteenth and seventeenth centuries, a mutation sadly ignored by the author.

*****

One leaves this book down with a deep feeling of disappointment. It never really lives up to its title and it never addresses the fundamental questions raised by its thesis or methodology. Its terms of reference as encapsulated in the title *(Gaelic mind ... Gaelic world)* are nowhere defined and there is a significant amount of imprecision and woolliness in their application. In fact, the 'Gaelic mind' of the title becomes the 'aristocratic Gaelic mentality' (p 51) - a totally different entity - in the course of the book and various terms are substituted loosely and indiscriminately for the 'Gaelic world': 'Gaelic aristocratic world' (p 6), 'Gaelic aristocratic lifestyle' (p 9), 'aristocratic Gaeldom' (p 9), 'bardic world' (p 21); the erroneous implication being that the terms are synonomous. The demise of this world is located both in 'the mid-seventeenth century' (p 37) and in 'the final decades of the seventeenth century' (p 35) but either obituary raises more questions than it answers.

Abbreviations

DER   Ó Raghallaigh, T, *Duanta Eoghain Ruaidh Mhic an Bhaird*, Gaillimh, 1930.

DMM   Mhág Craith, C, *Dán na mBráthar Mionúr*, Dublin, 1967.
FPP   O'Rahilly, C, *Five Seventeenth-Century Political Poems*, Dublin, 1952.
IBP   Bergin, O, *Irish Bardic Poetry*, Dublin, 1970.
MD   O'Rahilly, T F, *Measgra Dánta II*, Dublin, 1927.
ND   De Brún, P (*et al*), *Nua-dhuanaire I*, Dublin 1971.

REFERENCES

This essay was first published in *Eighteenth-Century Ireland*, Vol 7, Dublin, 1992, under the title of 'Poetry and Politics in Early Modern Ireland', and as a review of the book referred to in note 3 below. For a detailed and more comprehensive analysis of the issues discussed in this essay, see B Ó Buachalla's *Aisling Ghéar* (Dublin, 1996).

1   See, in particular, Brendan Bradshaw, 'Native Reaction to the Westward Enterprise: A Case-Study in Gaelic Ideology' in J H Andrews, N P Canny and P E Hair (eds), *The Westward Enterprise* (Liverpool, 1978), 65-80; N P Canny, 'The Formation of the Irish Mind: Religion, Politics and Gaelic Irish Literature 1550-1750,' in *Past and Present*, 95 (1982), 91-116; Tom Dunne, 'The Gaelic Response to the Conquest: The Evidence of the Poetry,' in *Studia Hibernica*, 20 (1980), 7-30; Breandán Ó Buachalla, 'Na Stíobhartaigh agus an tAos Léinn: Cing Séamas,' in *RIA Proceedings*, vol 83 C (1983), 81-134.

2   Of the works cited in n 1, only Dr Bradshaw's article is mentioned by Prof Aidan Clarke in the most recent survey of the historiography of the period; see A Clarke, R Gillespie, J McGuire. *A New History of Ireland: Bibliographical Supplement 1534-1691* (1991), 696-708.

3   Michelle O Riordan, *The Gaelic Mind and the Collapse of the Gaelic World* (Cork: University Press 1990).

4   For a different approach to bardic poetry, see K Simms, *From Kings to Warlords* (1987), p 4. 'Within each poem, most of the space is given up to certain stock motifs, repeatedly used in many periods and for many patrons ... Familiarity with the bardic style allows one to lay less emphasis on these sections of the poem and thus to focus with greater precision on the five or six stanzas containing an individual message'.

5   See, in particular, Dunne, *op cit.*

6   It is not immediately easy to assess the representative nature of the author's choice of poems as no index of first lines is provided - a regrettable omission.

7   *Mo thruaighe mar táid Gaoidhil*, ed MD 54 §§3, 8, 10, 12, 17, 20, 23. Later in the book, the author refers again to this poem and provides the following synopsis: 'Another poem ascribed to Fear Flatha Ó Gnímh beginning *Mo thruaighe mar táid Gaoidhil* deals with the same theme; Ireland is dead, her lands are held by foreigners, her fields are empty, her poets silent' (p 124).

8   See T Ó Donnchadha (ed), *Leabhar Cloinne Aodha Buidhe* (Dublin, 1931); C McGrath, 'Ollamh Cloinne Aodha Buidhe', *Éigse*, 7 (1953), 126-7; B Cunningham & R Gillespie, 'The East Ulster Bardic Family of Ó Gnímh', *Éigse*, 20 (1984), 106-14.

9   DMM 28 §§5-6.

10   This was a crucial concept in informing the attitude of the literati to Charles II in the period 1650-60 and, more particularly, to James II and James III after 1690. An instance of the term occurs in a poem discussed by the author (p 278) but its significance is neither noted nor discussed. Earlier examples occur in D Greene (ed), *Duanaire Méig Uidhir* (Dublin, 1972) 2§6; *Éigse* 15 (1973) 45 §57; DMM 24 §18, 38 §64, 39 §100. Dr Katharine Simms has pointed out that 'by the early fifteenth century the Irish themselves became conscious of a distinction between their own local "kings" and the heads of evolving nation-states in the rest of Europe' (K Simms, *op cit*, p 38).

11   Cf: 'As the poem appears to he an outspoken comment on contemporary events it is of considerable historical interest' (Ó Cuív, *op cit*, 261). For other early manifestations of an awareness of change (particularly in the religious sphere) see the scribal colophons in RIA MSS 23 P 16 (1554) 190, 24 P 14 (1578) 134.

12   Bradshaw, *op cit*, pp 66, 78.

13   The presence of the concept has been claimed for seventeenth-century sources, however. The two poets alluded to are Flann mac

Eoghain Meic Craith and Fear Gan Ainm mhac Eochadha, two minor poets.

14 See pp 19, 21-6, 48, 60, 68-9, 80, 91,96-118, 120-23, 175.

15 Cf: 'Poems from different areas and periods reveal varying attitudes towards the Anglo-Irish colony: hostility, apathy, or even on occasion, positive friendship' (Simms, *op cit*, p 5).

16 J C McErlean (ed), *Duanaire Dháibhidh Uí Bhruadair* III (London, 1917), p 65; as McErlean notes *(ibid)*, the poem has been called 'an ostensible panegyric of Queen Elizabeth' by Standish Hayes O'Grady.

17 See, for instance: 'On his accession, the Cypriotes [Irish] who, in the assertion of their liberties, had, both before his days and after, been involved in perpetual war with the Cilicians [English], when they saw on the throne a Monarch of their own race and blood, at once unhesitatingly submitted to their compatriot', C O'Kelly, *Macariae Excidium or the Destruction of Cyprus*, ed J C O'Callaghan (London, 1850), 7-8; cf also J. Lynch, *Cambrensis eversus* (St Malo, 1662), §§247-7.

18 See H Erskine-Hill, 'Literature and the Jacobite Cause', *Modern Language Studies*, 9, III (1979), 15-28; J R Moore, 'Windsor Forest and William III' *Modern Language Notes*, 66 (1951), 451-4; W Myers, *Dryden* (London, 1973), p 139.

19 For the concept and its application, see L Martines, *Society and History in English Renaissance Verse* (Oxford, 1987).

20 To take but one example, the fact that members of some of the leading learned families practised their professional skills in post-Reformation Ireland as religious or secular priests is not discussed nor is its (perceived/potential) impact on Irish literature examined.

21 Surprisingly, the author does not include in her study 'Do chuala scéal do chéas gach ló mé' (ND 26) which obviously belongs to the series, whereas she does include Haicéad's 'Múscail do mhisneach, a Bhanbha' which in metre, theme and diction is totally different and does not belong to the same series.

22 'Mór antrom Inse Banbha', ed E C Mac Giolla Eáin, *Dánta, Amhráin is Caointe Sheathrúin Céitinn* (Dublin, 1900), 62-7.

23 Some versions read: 'Barrys, Browns, Burkes, Lacys'.

24 Text: *den Ghallfhuil Ghaelaigh* 'of the foreign Irish blood'.

25 I use 'voice' here, as it is used in modem literary criticism, to denote the personality a rhetoric represents.

3. THE ULSTER RISING OF 1641 *

BRENDAN BRADSHAW

Revising the 'Risings' has been a major preoccupation of historians of Ireland, ever since the subject achieved the status of an academic, university-based discipline there in the decade or so immediately following the establishment of the Free State in 1922. The object of the exercise has been to debunk the interpretation of Irish history as a long struggle for national liberation, conducted by means of a succession of rebellions or uprisings, dating back to the medieval conquest of the island by the entrepreneurial vassals of Henry II in the later twelfth century. That interpretation was enshrined in the Proclamation of the Republic by the rebels of 1916, and it subsequently assumed the status of holy writ on the accession to power of the disciples of the martyred leaders in 1922.

The revisionist enterprise falls into two phases. The earlier period might be characterized as its age of original innocence. The pioneers, imbued with simple faith in scientific history, set out to investigate the course of Irish history, assured that the past 'as it really was' - in Leopold von Ranke's phrase - would reveal itself to the impartial investigator of the documentary sources, and that by this means the nationalist epic would be exposed as an ideologically motivated myth. Their mentor was the up-and-coming Herbert Butterfield, whose manifesto, *The Whig Interpretation of History* (1931), on behalf of value-free and 'past-centred' history - history 'for its own sake' - was taken

---

* This essay first appeared as a review of *Ulster 1641 - Aspects of the Rising*, Brian MacCuarta (ed), 1993.

to address the state of the art in Ireland quite as importunately as in England: history had been traduced by the Catholic nationalists now in power in the Free State, in the same way as liberal Protestant nationalists had traduced it in England to underwrite Britain's Whig constitution.

In the 1970s, this disinterested pursuit acquired a consciously aggressive anti-nationalist orientation, largely in response to the Northern troubles. A new generation of historians, prominent among them Conor Cruise O'Brien and F S L Lyons, dismayed by the resurgence of militant nationalism, and convinced that nationalistically biased history, especially the myth of a historic liberation struggle, continued to subserve an ideology of militant republicanism, proceeded to place revisionism as such at the top of the historical agenda. In response to such high-profile advocacy, revisionism came to enjoy a vogue within the profession, such that, by the mid-1980s, Roy Foster, the doyen of a younger generation again, could famously claim - or infamously as the viewpoint might be - 'we are all revisionists now'.

In the event, the claim proved premature. Already protesting voices were being raised at symposia and conferences. In 1989, in an article for the profession's in-house journal, *Irish Historical Studies,* I argued that the project of a scientific-revisionist history was vitiated from the outset by reliance on Herbert Butterfield's formula. The Olympian detachment he prescribes defies the human cognitive processes. Furthermore, 'history for its own sake', 'past-centred history', is morally objectionable as a retreat to the ivory tower and an abdication of the special public function of the historian: to promote social understanding of how the community has got to where it is. As a strategy for the investigation of the Irish past, Butterfield's formula made for both bad history and a bad social therapy. Bad history, because what resulted was a revisionist anti-myth set up against the nationalist one. The great patriots, entered for veneration in the nationalist canon, emerged from the devil's advocacy of the revisionists as a rogues' gallery with the gracelessness of power-hungry megalomaniacs and nincompoops. More objectionably, the catastrophic dimension of Irish history - conquest, colonization, dispossession, religious and social discrimination, immiseration - was subjected to a process of normalization and, indeed, tacit evasion, designed to rid Irish history of its legacy of bitterness. And bad history resulted in bad social therapy. As Roy Foster disconsolately admitted, addressing the Royal Historical Society in 1982, the effect of revisionism has been to open up a credibility gap between the academic historians and the Irish public. The public has failed in Foster's phrase to 'turn the corner' with the academics, because they sense that to do so would be to turn their backs on the Irish historical experience 'as it really was'.

Set in that context, the propensity of the Rising of 1641 to raise an academic barney will be appreciated. The debate acquires a peculiar intensity, however, because of the way the Rising continues to resonate divisively in the historical consciousness of the two Ulster communities. One source of recrimination relates to the question of origins, specifically whether the Rising is to be seen as a response to the Ulster Plantation thirty years earlier, the episode to which the loyalist community traces its roots and the nationalist community the opening chapter of its long history of immiseration. A second is the subject of the atrocities perpetrated by the Catholic rebels in 1641-2. What weight is to be given to the popular Protestant perception of them as the first act of genocide attempted by the natives, an attempt to be repeated time and again into modern times? On the other side, the question of the significance of the Rebellion in ideological terms arises. Was it the first of the great nationalist rebellions of the modern period, the first major attempt to throw off the yoke of British oppression in the aftermath of the Tudor conquest, or was it merely a backward-looking peasant fury? Finally, the new, so-called British history, the 'history of the Atlantic Archipelago' - John Pocock's preferred coinage - makes the cocktail still more explosive. What light does the Rising throw on the British Odyssey, on the unification process that began - however painfully and gradually - with the accession of the Scottish Stuarts to the throne of England and culminated in the establishment of the United Kingdom?

In projecting the collection of studies under review, its editor, Brian Mac Cuarta, was evidently much exercised by the divisive legacy bequeathed by the Rising to modern Ireland. This was so, first, because of his public concern as a historian with a special interest in the social consequences of early seventeenth-century plantation. Second, as is tacitly indicated by the eirenic foreword contributed by the Church of Ireland's Archbishop of Armagh, Robert Eames, Mac Cuarta's concern arose from his pastoral involvement as a Jesuit in an ecumenical mission of reconciliation located in the environs of Portadown, the scene of the most notorious massacre of the Rising. It is gratifying therefore to report that the editor is not only the initiator of the first full-scale investigation of the subject for seventy-four years, but he is also the author of a masterly introduction that shows him to be too sensible a historian and too clear-headed an ecumenist to be seduced by revisionism as a panacea for the Rising's bitter legacy. Regrettably, the substantive essays in *Ulster 1641: Aspects of the Rising* afford less gratification. Although researched and written at the highest level of professional competence, the collective achievement falls short of expectations. It represents a missed opportunity to break the mould. And to compound the disappointment, the miss must be ascribed in no small way to the failure of a number of Mac Cuarta's collaborators to show as much discernment as he does in regard to the supposedly ameliorative properties of revisionism.

To return to the question of the origins of the Rising, it is dismaying to find Raymond Gillespie still hammering home Aidan Clarke's thesis that the Ulster Rising came as a 'bolt from the blue'. This thesis was first put forward twenty-four years ago in Clarke's contribution to the otherwise much controverted subject of the 'general European crisis'; [†] and it needs to be reconsidered all the more urgently in the light of the accolade recently awarded it by Conrad Russell as 'a more extreme form of revisionism than I have ever attempted for England'. Untroubled by doubts, Gillespie blames the collapse of local government in Ulster at the onset of rebellion on the 'totally unexpected' nature of the disruption. Proceeding from there by means of an analytical *non sequitur,* he represents the Rising as an untoward convulsion, brought on by that factotum of the empiricists' explanatory model of popular revolt, socio-economic crisis - the familiar conjuncture of invariable variables, economic recession, dearth and unprecedented pressure by central government on local resources. By this means, Gillespie is able to take the appearance of stability in the preceding decade or so for reality and to depict the situation in Ulster in the aftermath of the Plantation as one of increasing normalization. 'Local accommodations' between settlers and natives were the order of the day, he suggests. The natives had reconciled themselves to making

---

[†] *Past and Present,* no 48, 1970.

the most of the crumbs that came their way, either as 'deserving Irish', assigned lands on the infertile margins, or as tenants paying exorbitant rents to the new owners, often for lands of which their own sept had been dispossessed and, in any case, which they now leased on substantially less advantageous terms than neighbouring tenants introduced from Scotland and the north of England. Totally satisfied by this account of affairs, Gillespie declines to follow the lead of evidence that points towards a deeply restive native community rife with conspiracy for the overthrow of the new order.

Hilary Simms's case-study of the *mentalité* of the rebels follows Gillespie's lead. Examining the motivation of the rebels in the course of an analysis of the Armagh depositions - the reports on the atrocities gathered by special commissioners at the time - she reports that, however the leaders may have been motivated, political considerations were not significant at the local level. There, rebellion was driven by sheer economic opportunism: by the opportunities it offered for plunder, blackmail and the remission of debt - this last by the grotesque expedient of writing off the creditor.

Yet Simms's testimony doesn't quite dispose of the issue. The evidence she adduces is tenuous and circumstantial: merely that the depositions often reveal a 'relationship of inequality' between the assailants and their victims, as tenants and landlords, servants and masters, debtors and creditors. More damagingly, she totally ignores the evidence that points in another direction, failing to take into account the implications of the ritualistic and symbolic character of so much of the violence perpetrated - the stripping of victims without sexual molestation, the burning of bibles, the desecration of Protestant places of worship. Viewed in that context, Simms's socio-economic thesis, like that of Gillespie, involves an analytical *non sequitur*. The readiness of the rebels to avail themselves of the opportunity of economic betterment does not rule out political or ideological considerations from their calculations.

Gillespie's lead is followed even more emphatically by Michelle O Riordan in her formidably erudite case-study of 'the native Ulster *mentalité* as revealed in Gaelic sources, 1600-50'. Her thesis is predicated on the astonishing failure, as she reports, of the cataclysm of conquest and colonization to register as such in native literary sources, not even, most astoundingly, in the vast corpus of political verse yielded by the genre of bardic eulogy, nor in the annalistic and antiquarian lore that purported to chronicle the history of the period. The key to the puzzle, she finds, is the peculiar state of stasis in which the native community perceived its political world to be suspended. This perception was moulded, she explains, by the bardic order - the native community's cultural priesthood - as a means of reconciling the tension between the reality and the ideal in the transmission of status and power in the heroic world of native dynastic politics. The bardic mediation took the form of the classical eulogy through which the *fait accompli* achieved by force was legitimated by acclaiming the victor as senior and best of the sept, in accordance with the law of tanistry. So O Riordan's contention is that the puzzling failure of the native literati to register the cataclysm of conquest and colonization is explained quite simply by their lack of the mental equipment to do so. In a word, 'normality' summarizes O Riordan's account of the native mental environment in the period preceding the Rising. On her reading of the native sources, the conquest and its sequel, the Ulster Plantation, could not have generated the grievances that propelled the natives into rebellion; so far as they were concerned, conquest and colonization as such never really happened. O Riordan's account of the native *mentalité* seems not only to clinch the case for the 'bolt from the blue' thesis, but also to dispose of the twin pillar of the nationalist interpretation: the notion that the Rising was fuelled by a burgeoning ideology of 'faith and fatherland'.

That cherished assumption is dismissed in O Riordan's account as a classic example of the anachronistic fantasies by which nationalist historians have been seduced in consequence of their predilection for reading history backwards. Starting from the other end, she has discovered, as might be expected, that the native *mentalité* conformed to the typology devised by historical anthropologists for characterizing the traditionalist outlook of pre-modern, rural, lineage societies generally. Localized, kin-centred and backward-looking, the mental horizons of the native Ulster community did not as yet comprehend the 'modern' concepts of nationality and confessional identity. Thus by removing 'modernity' beyond the purview of the rebels, whether expressed as a consciousness of conquest and colonization or as an ideology of 'faith and fatherland', O Riordan seems to clinch the case for the revisionist interpretation of the Rising.

The case O Riordan argues reiterates the thesis she had already presented in respect of the Gaelic community as a whole in her monograph of 1990, *The Gaelic Mind and the Collapse of the Gaelic World Order*. The case as elaborated there was dismantled systematically and in detail in two comprehensive critical reviews by scholars no less practised than she, to say the least, in handling the recalcitrant material.* The methodological flaws that then vitiated

---

* Breandán Ó Buachalla in *Eighteenth-Century Ireland*, 7, 1992, (see chapter 2) and Marc Caball in *Cambridge Medieval Celtic Studies*, 24, 1993.

O Riordan's analysis must be passed over here, apart from noting two principal sources of confusion: a uni-dimensional focus or tunnel vision and a susceptibility to modish literary theory stemming from the structuralist philosophy of Claude Levi-Strauss. As to substance, the diamond point is that the native literature does in fact register the cataclysm of conquest and colonization; it frequently develops the analogy between the plight of the downcast Irish and that of the Israelites wandering in the desert, and assumes a Messianic note in expressing the hope of deliverance through the emergence of a leader like Moses. Second, the literature reflects an associated mind-shift of radical dimensions. The horizons of the literati extend beyond the kin and the locality to the community of the whole island. Third, in conjunction, a new community consciousness is articulated: the collectivity is defined not in ethnic but in national terms; thus the two historic ethnic communities of the island, the Gaelic *(Gaeil)* and Anglo-Normans *(Gaill),* now styled Old English *(Sean-Ghaill),* are affirmed as one race, the Irish *(Éireannaigh).* Conversely, the new planters are now consigned to the status of foreigners - the alien others - as New English *(Nua Ghaill).* Fourth, the common identity of the Irish is predicated not only on their common origin as the historic inhabitants of the island but on a shared religious faith as Catholics *(Catailici),* distinguishing them in this respect again from the New English heretics, followers of Luther and Calvin. Finally, the cult of the Stuarts, which O Riordan takes to import the acceptance of the *fait accompli,* functions, on the contrary, as a vehicle through which to express the aspiration for its reversal: the Stuarts are celebrated as scions of the ancient Irish high-kings, in the manner of the Welsh bards eulogizing the Tudors, as the champions who will deliver the Irish from Saxon oppression. Presumably, the implications of all of this for O Riordan's thesis, and more crucially for the revisionist interpretation of the Rising, need not be laboured. An exploration of the mental environment that conditioned the rebellion, it turns out, serves not to put the final seal on the door closed by Aidan Clarke twenty-four years ago. The effect is rather to blow the door wide open and to inaugurate a post-revisionist phase in the interpretation of the Rising.

Some suggestions may be made for a post-revisionist agenda, prompted by a cursory review of the remaining essays in the collection. The starting-point is signposted in John McCavitt's valuable study of the Ulster Plantation. It does so by providing a tacit corrective to recent revisionist attempts to normalize that episode by setting the 'event' in the context of long-term conditioning structural forces: the 'push' of population pressure in the north of England and Lowland Scotland reciprocated by the 'pull' of easily accessible, sparsely inhabited and under-exploited cultivable land in the North of Ireland. Tacitly redirecting attention to the uniqueness of the event itself, McCavitt highlights the political exigencies to which it was responding: notably Ireland's new strategic importance, after replacing Scotland as the back door through which an invasion of England was likely to be mounted. He quotes the tragically prophetic warning of Lord Deputy Chichester of the counter-productive consequences likely to accrue from the radical scheme which superseded his own modest proposal. No humanitarian but a hard-headed politician, Chichester warned that the natives would 'kindle a new fire in those parts at one time or another if they be not well looked to or provided for in reasonable measure'. Unfortunately, McCavitt loses the courage of his convictions in concluding nevertheless - invoking the authority of Clarke - that 'the 1641 Rising cannot be explained in simplistic terms as *the* inevitable product of the iniquities of the Ulster Plantation'.

Fair enough. But that begs the question: even if the nationalists were wrong to postulate the iniquities of the Plantation as a sufficient explanation of the origins of the 1641 Rising, are those iniquities nevertheless a necessary and indeed a central dimension of such an explanation?

Moving back to the debatable ground of *mentalité*, Gráinne Henry valuably supplements the testimony already considered in raising afresh the question of the values and attitudes brought to bear by the rebels. Her essay sets out to explore the origins of a historical phenomenon of major significance for the course of Irish history through the modern period: the Irish Diaspora. Henry charts the formation across Europe, under the benign auspices of its Catholic rulers, of communities of dispossessed or in any case disenchanted exiles and traces the development of the expatriate 'faith and fatherland' ethos that came to characterize them. More importantly for present purposes, she also elaborates the communications network through which the expatriates maintained contact with the homeland. Henry emphasizes the militancy that characterized the expatriate ideology of faith and fatherland and singles out the missionizing of the friars as a medium by which the same militancy was injected into the homegrown variety. Perhaps it is to ask too much that having pressed her case even more forcefully than McCavitt, she should clinch the argument by drawing attention to its implications for the revisionist interpretation of the Rising. Be that as it may, it becomes clearer than ever that the *mentalité* of the native Ulster community in the early seventeenth century is in urgent need of revisitation as a factor in conditioning the outbreak and sustaining the momentum of the rebellion.

As for the atrocities, it should be emphasised immediately that it would form no part of a post-revisionist agenda to demythologize that gruesome episode. Quite the contrary.

A case in point comes to mind on the occasion of a symposium held in Portadown to mark the 350th anniversary of the Rising in 1991. An insouciant revisionist chose the occasion to urge the mainly Protestant audience to believe that the painful memory which haunted the collective consciousness of Ulster Protestants was implanted not by an unfortunate incident in the remote past but by the agitations of unscrupulous demagogues in the nineteenth century conjuring up the spectre of the green peril from history. Happily none of the contributors to the present volume can be accused of such insouciance. Indeed, Jacqueline Hill provides a valuable corrective. She traces the troublesome afterlife of the horror and explains the circumstances in which it gave place in the eighteenth century to 'the Boyne and King Billy' as the central event in the foundation legend of the community, while remaining the fulcrum of the community's siege mentality - the memory that taught it to espouse eternal vigilance as the condition of mere survival.

More remains to be done, however, as the contributions of two of the most respected authorities on the subject show. One is by the master himself, Aidan Clarke. His study of the '1641 Rebellion and Anti-Popery in Ireland' focuses centrally on the atrocities as they affected Protestant perceptions of the native community. The trouble is partly that Clarke's thesis rests on a case-study of doubtful expository value. It is drawn from an analysis of a contemporary report prepared for the English parliament in 1642 which, he suggests, although unpublished and unknown, is to be taken to represent 'the more authentic colonial voice' over Sir John Temple's *The Irish Rebellion,* first published in 1646 and repeatedly thereafter into the twentieth century, and always regarded as the standard Protestant version. Even more problematical is the conclusion to which the analysis of his preferred source leads him. He argues that the perception of the natives moulded by the massacres in the collective consciousness of the colonists was one in which 'the apparatus of the pope and his minions was relegated to an opportunist rather than an instrumental role'; these were subordinated to 'a local and secular demonology', formulated by colonists of a humanist bent in the sixteenth century. It is hard to believe so, given the prominence accorded the 'pope and his minions' in the anti-Irish rhetoric of Ulster Protestants then and ever since - as witness Ian Paisley. There is a further problem that Clarke seems to be engaging (without saying so) in the academic pastime which he describes elsewhere as floating 'trial balloons': an innocuous enough hobby, no doubt, except that it has had the effect when indulged in by Clarke in the past, such is his justifiably formidable scholarly reputation, of luring unduly 'reverential' readers up a blind alley - as witness Gillespie, Simms, O Riordan, McCavitt and Conrad Russell. Above all, Clarke's contribution, though conducted at a characteristically sophisticated level of scholastic fine-tuning, fails to engage with the horror of the experience as it impacted on the consciousness of the settler community, lodging there as an ineradicable memory which has haunted Ulster Protestants ever since.

The same must be said of Toby Barnard's bibliographical essay. His elegant and wide-ranging survey of the literature - from the original hysterical reports, through the polemical jousts of Catholic and Protestant antiquarians to the studies of professional historians more latterly - is presented as a cautionary tale of the way in which 'the regular revisiting of 1641, though it owed something to supposed improvements in historical methods, was usually prompted by, and in its turn contributed to, contemporary grudges'. The point is well made and duly taken. Nevertheless, Barnard's story tapers off with an account of the unedifying wrangle between two eminent Victorians, J A Froude and John Gilbert. No more than a cursory glance is thrown in the direction of more recent scholarship except for (who else but?) Aidan Clarke, who is singled out for final commendation. The question that most urgently needs to be addressed by historians in the present distressed circumstances is never raised. Given that the myth of the massacres has turned out on scholarly investigation to contain much more than a kernel of truth, how is that past 'as it really was' to be explained in a way that may assist the present-day Ulster Protestant community to live with the painful memory? That challenge confronts historians of the post-revisionist phase no less urgently than does the catastrophic history of Ulster's Catholic community.

The two remaining essays in the collection raise the question of the significance of the Rising in the context of the new British history. If, as seems likely, the 'bolt from the blue' thesis fails to withstand reconsideration, the effect will be to redound on Conrad Russell's 'less extreme' version of the same thesis already being pummelled by post-revisionists as Russell applies it to the outbreak of the civil war in England between supporters of the king and of Parliament. In addition, the relevance of the Rising to the new British history relates to an issue far more central to that enterprise.

This emerges from Michael Percevall-Maxwell's careful analysis of the place of the Rising in precipitating the War of the Three Kingdoms. The effect is to highlight its crucial function in reversing the process of healing and settling, initiated in the aftermath of the execution of Strafford, between King Charles I and the political élites of his three kingdoms - including the Old English in Ireland. Were it not for the Ulster Rising, Percevall-Maxwell persuasively argues, no such conflagration would have occurred. The effect of this analysis, in turn, though Percevall-Maxwell does not seem to notice, is to draw attention to the emerging role of Ireland in the Odyssey of the British polity that began with the accession of the Scottish Stuarts to the throne of England. From this point onwards, Ireland was to emerge increasingly as the destabilizing element in the multiple polity ruled by the King of England, the only component of the multinational conglomerate to persist in resisting integration within the unitary state into which the Atlantic Archipelago was now evolving. In short, the significance of the Rising in the context of the new British history in the first instance is to draw attention to the place occupied by Ireland within that history as *the* British Problem.

The interest of the final essay in the collection is to suggest a conceptual frame within which the problematical history of Ireland in the Odyssey of the British polity might be explored. Phil Kilroy is concerned to delineate the religious ethos that came to characterize the reformed Church of Ireland and to outline the development in Ulster, within the institutional frame of the established Church, of a presbyterizing movement that was to result after the Restoration in the withdrawal into dissent of the great majority of Ulster Protestants. However, set in the British context - which is not Kilroy's concern - the effect of the analysis is to delineate the basis on which Ireland emerged as an anomaly not only within the British conglomerate but within the conglomerate of confessional states that defined the political configuration of post-Reformation Europe. This resulted from the exclusive identification of the colonists in the course of the early seventeenth century with the Calvinistic Protestantism espoused by the inhabitants of the British conglomerate generally and the abandonment of the colonized natives to the proscribed Catholicism of the Counter-Reformation. Set in the context of the British conglomerate then, Ireland came to assume a doubly anomalous aspect in the course of the early seventeenth century: a kingdom that also constituted the first colony of the British Empire, and one that comprised a majority of expropriated, native Catholics

The effect of the process of religious delineation that occurred in early seventeenth-century Ireland was to absorb the conjoined grievances of the majority population - land and religion - into a political grievance, the downgraded status of the island from autonomous kingdom to appended colony. In that light, the larger implication of the case argued throughout this review concerning the origins of the Ulster Rising need scarcely be emphasized. The linked grievances of land and religion, subsumed under the political one relating to the treatment of Ireland as a colony, hold the key to the Ulster Rising in 1641. And it is because of this treatment that Ireland emerged as the destabilizing element within the British conglomerate. To explore the implications of the Rising in those terms is perhaps the most urgent task for the agenda that awaits attention in the post-revisionist phase of interpretation.[†]

[†] This review first appeared in *The Times Literary Supplement*, 14 October 1994.

4. SCIENCE, TECHNOLOGY & NATIONALITY

ROY JOHNSTON

What follows is an agenda for what I think historians should be looking at, if they are to help us to gain an understanding of how societies develop national identities, and how nations develop economic viability through the mastery of productive processes which depend increasingly on the application of science-based technologies.

Bacon and the Royal Society

What may be called the Baconian[1] model, with a systematic organised approach to the wresting of secrets from nature, was embodied in the Royal Society at is foundation. The philosophy from the start was that 'knowledge is power' and the strategic interests of the central State were at the top of the agenda. Anyone who doubts the English imperial role of the early Royal Society and the Baconian model should read the 'plan for Ireland' devised by Sir William Petty who, along with Newton and Boyle, was among the founding fathers.

Boyle's father was the Earl of Cork who implemented the Munster plantation under Elizabeth, in which context Edmund Spenser fell foul of the unruly aboriginals who, rejecting the process, burned him out. Boyle's Irish roots were like the Duke of Wellington's ('being born in a stable

---

[1] Sir Francis Bacon: Elizabethan politician; author of *Novum Organum*, widely regarded in the West as the foundation text of the 'scientific method'. This, however, is increasingly disputed in the Third World: a collection of United Nations University essays edited by Ashis Nandy contains a critical analysis by J K Bajaj.

does not make one a horse'). Boyle, however, has a role in the culture of science in Ireland, in that he is commemorated with a Boyle Medal, issued periodically as a mark of esteem by the Irish scientific establishment, since it was initiated by Joly [2] in 1898. I will return to this, to explain what I think is its significance.

The Baconian model was the pattern for the imperial scientific establishments of France, Prussia, Russia, Austro-Hungary, indeed of all European States. There was in all cases a usually quite explicit Faustian pact with the military establishments, which contributed to the painful way in which European history has evolved.

Mini-Baconian systems on the English model popped up in Scotland and in Ireland (not to my knowledge in Wales). There was the Royal Society of Edinburgh; in Dublin there was the Royal Dublin Society (RDS) in 1731 and then the Royal Irish Academy (RIA) in 1784. These two (consciously Baconian) bodies were at the core of the process of the development of the scientific and technological potential for the existence of the Irish nation. Their ultimate failure to achieve an impact on the thinking of the intellectual leadership of the Irish revolution in the 1900s is at the root of the contemporary cultural gap. Why was this?

---

[2] John Joly FRS (Fellow of the Royal Society), geologist and physicist, was active from the 1890s to the 1920s in Trinity College Dublin; first physicist to come up with a realistic estimate of the age of the earth, based on radioactive decay processes; discoverer of the element samarium; inventor of a colour photographic process; was actively involved in the defence of TCD during the 1916 Rising.

America and France

The role of Benjamin Franklin in America illustrates how the scientist who is a long way from the core of scientific culture can contribute. He became a printer/editor/publisher, popularised useful technologies (like the 'Franklin stove' without which it would have been difficult to survive the New England winter) and helped to make the political revolution. He had to go that road, because the road to peer-esteem via core-recognition was blocked to him by the width of the Atlantic.

When American democratic ideas were taken up in France, reinforcing the European Enlightenment, there was already in existence a central imperial State, with Baconian institutions, which influenced the flavour of the democratic revolutionary aftermath, pushing it towards the Bonapartist (proto-Stalinist) model. This favoured scientific technology, under the Faustian pact, and the École Polytechnique became the focus of the European scientific core, with England relegated to fringe status. (The focus later shifts to Germany, and then in this century to the USA, but this is another story, with which scientists will be familiar).

In Ireland and Scotland in the 1790s the link with the European core was closer than it was in the case of the US, and there was mobility of people. French influence on science in Scotland (the 'Scottish Enlightenment') and Ireland was considerable, and the English were leapfrogged. In Ireland by the 1800s the RDS was consciously on the way to becoming a technological university on the École Polytechnique model.[3] Had the United Irishmen established

[3] Higgins' course in industrial chemistry in the RDS was internationally famous; Kirwan in Dublin was in contact with Lavoisier in France and promoted the new chemistry, while Priestly in

their pluralist democratic republic in the 1790s, under American and French political influence, they would have had access to European core-quality science, organised as such, on the Baconian model.

Kane and Industrial Resources

There was an apostolic succession from this heroic epoch up to the Parnellite Home Rule period, embodied in the Kane family, father and son. The father, after participating in the 1798 republican uprising, went on the run to France, where he studied chemistry. He came back to Dublin when the dust had settled, and set up the first embodiment of the Gay-Lussac process (for the production of sulphuric acid) outside France. The son, who subsequently became famous as Sir Robert Kane, was President of the Royal Irish Academy in the Parnell epoch.

Kane picked up chemistry from the Higgins RDS lectures after school. He went to pursue his scientific studies in Germany and in 1829 discovered a manganese arsenide in Saxony, which was named Kaneite.

He went on to discover the ethyl radical, and was able to claim priority over Liebig, with whom he subsequently worked in Giessen in 1836. He worked in the RDS, mostly on organic chemistry; his process for converting acetone to mesitylene was the first to build a ring from a chain, and was acclaimed by Berzelius. In 1840 he became editor of the Philosophical Magazine of the Royal Society, and in 1849 became an Fellow thereof. Kane's Elements of Chemistry 1840-41 has 1200 pages and 200 wood-cuts. Faraday introduced it to the Army course at Woolwich, and the

---

England was still supporting the phlogiston theory of combustion.

American edition in 1843 was adopted as the US standard university course.

Kane's *Industrial Resources of Ireland* was published in 1843. This was the bible of Irish national techno-economic development for the next century, remaining so right up to de Valera's time, long after the technologies he outlined had become obsolete or irrelevant. It is one of the great Irish 'might-have-beens': if the Young Irelanders had succeeded, and the effects of the Famine contained by a sympathetic national State, Kane's ideas would have had some chance of being realised.

'Godless Colleges'

Kane became the President of Queen's College Cork on its foundation in 1846. He was more than just a 'token Catholic'; he was a figure of European stature who had come up despite the Protestant monopoly of higher education. The Queen's Colleges in Cork, Galway and Belfast were, however, condemned by Cardinal Cullen, and the Catholic establishment held out for a 'Catholic University'. This blocked access to higher education for the rising Catholic middle class for two generations, until the NUI was set up in 1906. The effect of this on the development of access to core-European scientific and technolgical culture in the Irish national context was devastating. It resulted in the virtual confinement of scientific culture into a Protestant colonial ghetto, though before the 1900s occasional Catholics filtered in, mostly via education abroad. (The analogue in modern times would be if there had been a demand in South Africa for a segregated black university!)

The consequence of this ban was that the key Baconian institutions, the RDS and the RIA, remained as the intellectual foci of the Protestant colonial nation: basically the landed gentry and the Trinity College élite, without enrichment from the rising Catholic middle classes.

Yet they did exist as the scientific foci of an Irish geographical entity, with an economic life, and a national potential. This could not help breaking through. The Protestant scientific élite were divided: some (like McCullagh, Haughton, Preston) looked to the emerging pluralistic geographical nation, with Davis and Parnell, others (like the Earl of Rosse, his son Parsons of steam turbine fame and Fitzgerald) to the then emerging and world-dominating British Empire. The full analysis of this contradiction remains to be done, but broadly speaking in the early 1880s the Academy was Home Rule inclined, under the leadership of the then ageing Kane, while the RDS focused the interests of those who looked to the Empire, led by Fitzgerald and Stoney.[4]

The extent of the frustrated potential of the Catholics for science is illustrated by the case of Callan, who was professor of physics in Maynooth, and had encountered Galvani and Volta when in Rome studying for the priesthood. He was practical and inventive, but in the Irish Protestant colonial scientific context was an outsider. He invented the induction coil, usually attributed to Rumkorff. Callan's priority was not generally established until an article in *Nature* in the 1950s. The effect of the Catholic ban

---

[4] G F Fitzgerald and his uncle G J Stoney were a formidable duo who dominated the RDS in the 1880s and 1890s. Fitzgerald is best known for his contribution to the understanding of the velocity of light in relativity theory; he came up with the 'Fitzgerald-Lorenz contraction' as the explanation of the null result of the Michelson-Morley experiment on 'ether drift'. The path from this led directly to Einstein. Both were FRSs. The RDS in those days was awash with FRSs.

on the 'Godless colleges' cannot be overestimated. If the Queen's Colleges had been allowed to thrive, Callan would have been part of a vibrant nation-wide scientific research community, with an inside track into electro-technology.

Publication Pattern

The Academy Proceedings has had a steady stream of papers from its foundation, at about the same rate, or at most slowly increasing. In recent times the exponential global scientific expansion has been taken up by the tendency to publish for peer-esteem in the specialist journals abroad.

Stoney and Fitzgerald in the 1890s foresaw this trend and tried to stem it, with an unsuccessful attempt to do a deal with Edinburgh against London, in the interests of local publication. (There was an embryonic national conscious-ness lurking there, even among the Baconian imperial élite).

The RDS, after its 'belle époque' with the French con-nection in the 1800s, had a publication hiatus until the 1850s, whereupon it started again, rising rapidly and peaking in the 1880s, when Fitzgerald led the walk-out from the Academy, and again in the 1910s, led by Joly. In its prime *RDS Proceedings* was peppered with papers by FRSs, and were in the mainstream of European cutting-edge technol-ogy; they were exchanged with all the main European scientific foci. This momentum continued up to the 1920s, and the bicentenary in 1932 was a gala event, attended by every member of the Free State Government; there was a scientific exhibition, and a ball. After this, however, RDS publications declined, and in the 1950s they were at the 1850 level. There was a revival in the Sixties and Seventies when the RDS was adopted by the rising Agricultural Science fraternity, but it has now declined again, and publication has virtually ceased.

A significant proportion of the papers published by the colonial scientific élite in the peak period of the 1910s was to do with the Faustian pact with the imperial military establishment. Sir Howard Grubb FRS was influential in the RDS at that time, and his optical works in Rathmines supplied the British Navy with gunsights, as well as the world with astronomical telescopes. There was also a significant amount of publication based on field-work done in India and elsewhere in the imperial context.

The setting up in 1898 of the Boyle Medal as a means of showing peer-esteem for scientific work done in Ireland can, I suggest, be interpreted as imperial triumphalism. Boyle was celebrated in the RDS as one of the Baconian founders of the Royal Society, rather than as someone of Irish origin (see Joly's RDS discourse on the occasion). Joly, who was the inheritor of Fitzgerald's mantle, would have been celebrating the defeat of Parnellite Home Rule, and the recovery of the RIA from nationalist domination.

The subsequent history of the Boyle Medal is of interest, and I hope to be able to analyse it in due course. It became for a period, post-1921, an indicator of good work of national significance, but as time went on, the means of identifying such good work became more difficult, as local publication went into decline.

In the 1930s an unsuccessful attempt was made to displace Boyle's name from the Medal, and substitute that of Kane; this was led by Felix Hackett, who was of the first flush of Catholic scientists who came though UCD, under McClelland.[5] Hackett, however, was scientifically in dis-

---

[5] McClelland and the Nolan brothers established a school of physical research dedicated to condensation nuclei in the atmosphere, which endures to this day. They published in the

credit, as having been associated with the N-ray canard [6] in the 1900s.

It is no good substituting 'being politically correct' for doing good science. The first flush of UCD people in the 1900s were enthusiasts and did much good work; in a situation when new things were being discovered and old paradigms overturned some errors of judgment are perhaps inevitable.

Post 1921 Faustian Pact?

The Irish Free State was not an imperial country, and did not have military aspirations. The traditional role for Baconian scientific institutions was in support of the major European imperial States.

The Irish mini-Baconian system was an offshoot of the British Empire; it has had its occasional dallyings with national aspirations on the American colonial pattern; it has helped to set up all the Baconian institutional trappings of European nation-statehood: the National Museum, National Library, Botanic Gardens, Ordnance Survey, Geological Survey etc. All these were in existence before the State was established. The infrastructure existed for the continuation of

---

Academy in the 1910s, at a time when the RDS was solidly imperial in its interests, thus in a sense reclaiming the Academy as a national focus, and picking up the Kane tradition. This school has persisted and is currently booming thanks to the increased international interest in the environment.

[6] Hackett F E; 'The Photometry of N-rays'; *Sci Trans* RDS Vol 8, 127-138. This work was subsequently exposed as fraudulent by R W Wood in Johns Hopkins in the USA. This may be regarded as an example of the 'cold fusion' type of phenomenon.

a vibrant scientific culture, and its conscious development towards the national interest.

What happened? Nothing. There was no attempt made to replace the imperial objectives of the old system with new national objectives, to develop a post-Baconian system in which science was dedicated to supporting the development of the new nation, and to serve the people. The infrastructure was simply allowed to atrophy, under a scientifically illiterate Civil Service.

This neglect persisted right up to the Sixties, when in the light of a somewhat scathing OECD Report the State set up a National Science Council (NSC).[7] This, however, was an appointed body, and science policy has since then developed on the basis of State centralism, with appointed boards etc.

The old Baconian institutions, with their basically healthy traditions of peer-review and democratic structures, have been allowed to persist with a somewhat nominal existence; they never assumed with the State in Ireland the status that the Royal Society has with the State in Britain.

Science and the Nation: Notes Towards a Model

I did promise a model. The foregoing is some of the background which suggests that a model is possible and

---

[7] *Science and Irish Economic Development*; 1964. The authors acknowledged positively the influence of J D Bernal FRS, whose classic 1939 book *The Social Function of Science* played a seminal role in science policy analysis, from a consciously Marxist angle. The Bernalist model was influential in the USSR and Eastern Europe. In the over-emphasis on the top-down role of the central State the Bernal model was, however, flawed, and science policy in Ireland shows signs of this parentage

relevant. I am not suggesting that what I now propose is in any sense complete.

I can begin by suggesting a rule for what will happen if scientists are not consciously involved in the nation-building process. The rule is that they will seek esteem within their discipline, and will publish to this end, and will migrate to the core where the action is. This would appear to be primarily the case with Wales, and also with Scotland, though perhaps less so, insofar as the existence of the Royal Society of Edinburgh acts as a national focus.

Despite the existence of an old-established Baconian institutional tradition in Ireland, this rule also holds, as scientific organisation has largely been allowed to atrophy, though for a time it looked as if there was enough of a critical mass to sustain local publication and esteem generation, and a status such as to make the State aware of science as an important factor.

There has to be a strong and transparent contract between the national movement, or the emerging national State, and the scientific and technological community, on the basis of mutual recognition and respect. This contract should avoid the Faustian role which is endemic in the Baconian tradition. We can perhaps define the science-State relationship as being 'post-Baconian', if the core of the arrangement is the concentration of scientific attention on building up the independent economic life of the emerging State, rather than on predation on neighbouring States.

The scientific and technological communities exist in the form of organisations, associations, institutions etc to which people adhere for the purpose of interaction with their peers, accreditation, information, contacts and so on.

If these exist, as autonomous entities, over a geographical area which is a candidate for recognition as a national State, then the scientific community may to that extent be considered 'national-minded'. It would then be in a position to organise itself over that geographical area, as a branch of an international or European institution. It is possible to talk about a 'national scientific community' with a conscious existence.

If such a situation exists, for each branch of science and technology, and if the organisations concerned are in a position to get together in the formulation of policy proposals, then we have a healthy situation, and the Government (or the national movement, in a pre-State situation) would have to listen.

This situation has never existed for Ireland since the State was founded. There had been the basis for its existence for a period under the British, when the RDS was in Leinster House, close to the Academy in Dawson Street.

There were, however, two channels (divide et impera): the Academy dealt with the Treasury, like the Royal Society and the Royal Society of Edinburgh, and the RDS dealt with the Department of Science and Arts (DSA) in Kensington. There was some exchange of ideas between the Academy channel and the Home Rule movement for a time, but virtually none in the period leading up to 1916. This is an important contributing factor to the current lack of appreciation of science in Irish culture.

Fitzgerald and Stoney [8] in the 1880s tried to unify the organisational structure, on the basis of a single Royal

---

[8] The details of the politics of this epoch need elaboration. Fitzgerald's motivation was primarily the development of a unified scientific lobby, to get things done. He went on to promote technical education in Dublin, and is counted among the founding fathers of the Dublin Institute of Technology. (For Stoney, see footnote 9.)

Society of Dublin, in which Academy members would have had Fellow status, and from which the old RDS agricultural interests would have been shed. This failed because Kane and the then Home Rule Academy leadership valued the status of the direct link with the Treasury and objected to being under the DSA.

The Irish State could have pulled this together, but it didn't. The Academy now deals with the Department of Education and Science, and the RDS is on its own, surviving on the income from the showground and exhibition halls.

In the Irish Republic the only unified body now is the Institution of Engineers of Ireland, which unites all engineering disciplines, and has successfully lobbied the Government for an Act defining the status of Chartered Engineer. The scientific community, however, is divided, some being Irish-based and some being London-oriented.

For a brief period in the 1960s the present writer acted as the secretary of a body which attempted to draw together the scientific and engineering interests to produce a policy document, in the aftermath of the OECD Report, proposing how the State should set up structures in response. This was not successful; the NSC was set up as an appointed body, State centralist paternalism reigns, and the democratic process is in abeyance.

However, more recently, the science community in Ireland has begun to get its act together via the Irish Research Scientists' Association of Ireland. The IRSA is in a position to lobby the Government and is beginning to be listened to by the Civil Service and State agencies. An important focal annual event is the Johnstone Stoney

Summer School [9] at which scientists and government representatives come together and listen to each other.[†]

---

[9] Stoney was Secretary of the Queen's Colleges, in which capacity he effectively lobbied the Government in London for resources for science. As a physicist, he contributed to the definitions of the basic electrical units and predicted the existence of a basic unit of electrical charge, estimating its size and naming it the 'electron' in 1891. It was subsequently discovered experimentally by J J Thomson of Cambridge in 1897. The centenaries of the electron were thus celebrated six years apart in Ireland and Britain by their respective scientific communities.

[†] This essay is based on an article in *Planet* (110, 1995, Aberystwyth).

5. THE ECONOMICS & POLITICS OF RAYMOND CROTTY

ANTHONY COUGHLAN

Raymond Crotty (1925-94) is the distinguished exception to the oft-made generalisation that while Ireland has made extraordinary contributions to English literature and drama, well out of proportion to its population size, it has produced little original work in economics or sociology. Crotty is one of the handful of Irish economists, past or present, who has any significant intellectual reputation outside Ireland. That reputation is likely to grow as people come to appreciate the importance of his discoveries in pastoral economics and their relevance to understanding the origin and development of civilisation.

Raymond Crotty's originality and insights were due in large part to the unconventional way in which he came to his subject. Most economists follow an orthodox educational and career path and lack practical experience of employment other than as professional economists in the economies they speculate about and prescribe for. Crotty was different. As he put it in his charming autobiography, *A Radical's Response,* written in 1988: 'Familiar situations can seem different when viewed from an unfamiliar perspective. Most social scientists are born and live their lives in what the marketing people refer to as social classes A and B. I appear to be the only economist who has earned a living for a prolonged period - from 1942 to 1961 - solely from farming in a former capitalist colony. This is also the sole occupation of perhaps as much as one third of the world's workforce.'

A 'townie' - Kilkenny is full of Crottys - he became interested in farming as a young man. He wanted to be a model farmer and studied for a time at the Albert Agriculture College, Dublin. In 1945, the year World War II ended, his father helped him buy a two-hundred acre farm near Kilkenny. The prudent course would have been to rent out most of it in 'conacre' for pasture and plough one-tenth of it. Instead he worked to increase his output per acre to around eight times the Irish average by means of intensive tillage, using farm machinery, investing in fertilisers and employing several men, borrowing from the bank to help with finance. This made him a model farmer by current official standards. Yet he did not make much money. He had modest margins compared to the very different regime of his neighbours, who seemed to get by with much less effort and investment, following traditional Irish 'dog and stick' farming methods, in which they watched their grass grow and their milch or beef cattle fatten.

Seven years of not very profitable farming on his own account gave Crotty the basic insight that in Irish circumstances, as he explained in his autobiography, 'It is not how much you get out, it's how little you put in that determines financial success or failure in Irish farming. ... Prices were lower and/or costs were higher in Ireland. Therefore, it was economically sensible not to use much of the higher cost inputs to produce much of the lower priced outputs. The secret was to see how little one could get away with spending and to let the output take care of itself.' Invited in the early 1950s to write a column for the *Irish Farmers Journal*, he began to think about wider economic and policy issues relating to farming.

Land Tax

Naturally, Ireland as a whole needed to maximize agricultural output, as being what the national interest and the social good demanded. But individual farmers had no interest in that. Many of them did best by minimising their inputs. Crotty recognised that it was fair and proper that farmers should be expected to contribute to the public purse in accordance with the amount of land they held rather than the use they made of it. Thus the one-hundred-acre man should contribute twice as much as the fifty-acre man. Yet he sometimes contributed less because of his low output per acre and inefficient use of land. Correspondence with former Fianna Fail Agriculture Minister Seán Moylan led Crotty to Henry George's famous book *Progress and Poverty,* published in the US in 1880. He was convinced by George's argument for taxing land in accordance with its extent and productivity in order to maximise output and appropriate the economic rent of land for the use of society.

In 1956 he abandoned tillage, laid off five of his six farm workers, bought some cows, aiming to get his income from their milk and calves, and embarked on the systematic study of economics. He first sat for GCE A-Levels, then enrolled at the London School of Economics for the external B Sc Econ degree. His aim was to write a book to explain why Irish farming was not making the contribution he believed it could and should make to national well-being, and to identify the measures necessary to change that.

Crotty was the first LSE external student to take mathematical economics in his degree, which he secured with honours. He then rented his farm and lived off the rent while undertaking postgraduate work at the LSE, securing an M Sc in Economics. This was followed by an appointment as lecturer in Agricultural Economics at the University of Wales, Aberystwyth. While there he wrote *Irish Agricultural Production, Its Volume and Structure* (1966), his first book, in which he set out his conclusions on Irish economic history:

The essence of my thought was that the land of Ireland belongs to the people of Ireland, equally to the entire people of Ireland. Property in Irish land had been a disaster for the nation ever since its creation by the confiscation of the clans' lands under the Tudor monarchs; and it continued to be so. Unless the Conquest could be undone by causing Irish land to be used efficiently and once more for the benefit of all the people, the Irish economy could not prosper. ... The necessary and sufficient condition for having Irish land operated efficiently on behalf of all the people is that it should be taxed to its full annual value. Land's annual value is broadly equivalent to the 'rack rents' that Anglo-Irish landlords extracted in the 19th century; or the competitive rents that Irish farmers exact for the one-tenth of all land that continues to be let out on yearly tenancies. The revenue from a tax on land would make it possible to reduce, or to remove, taxes on the inputs to and the outputs from land.

Ireland has six to seven times more arable land in proportion to its population size than any other European country. Land is therefore the country's principal natural advantage. The use that has been made of the very considerable income accruing to land has, therefore, been of great importance in determining the well-being of Irish society. The key to solving the country's traditional economic problem of high emigration and unemployment lies therefore, Crotty concluded, with managing its land resources and the potential revenue from them in such a way as to compensate for the economic disadvantages of Ireland's insular geography and small local population. For these disadvantages make much Irish manufacturing and service activity inherently more costly than in Britain or on the continent.

A revenue-maximizing land tax, imposed on rural and urban land - possibly exempting small-holdings for social reasons - should in principle ensure that only those best able to operate the land would continue to do so. The rest would be under pressure to retire, take up other work or rent out on long leases whatever land they could not efficiently operate themselves. A land tax should lower land prices and thereby help get land into the hands of young people better able to use it than the middle-aged, elderly or widowed farm-occupiers who currently own disproportionate amounts of Ireland's land. It would make for the more efficient use of land, raise agricultural output and provide the community with revenue to subsidise off-farm economic activity.

Instead of this happening, however, the opposite happened. Because in Ireland land ownership was absolute and people could use or neglect their land as they pleased - pursuing land intensive rather than labour intensive activity - much of the country's land produced as little as was possible for it under an Irish sky. The abolition of rates on land, vestigial land taxes, in the 1980s, made it even more valuable. Historically, Irish land values have tended continually to rise. This has made it ever harder for young active people who might use land more productively to become farmers. Irish public policy since the so-called 'Whitaker revolution' of the late 1950s, had operated to cheapen capital, subsidise capital investment and encourage the replacement of workers by machines. The higher taxes and public borrowing needed for this have made the employment of labour ever more expensive. Naturally, powerful interests stood to benefit from such policies - most obviously the owners of land and capital - while the discontented emigrated. Crotty contended that the solution to Ireland's emigration and unemployment problems therefore was to change the relative prices of land, labour and capital - to make land and capital more expensive by taxing them, and use the proceeds to subsidise the employment of labour, either directly or in the form of a national dividend that would give everyone in society a share in rising social productivity

Undoing the Conquest

For Crotty such measures would amount to the undoing of the Tudor and Cromwellian conquest of Ireland, which had instituted private property in land in a pastoral country inherently unsuited to it. He contended that what was needed to transform Irish 'undevelopment' into development 'involves essentially eliminating capitalist colonial privilege and its associated disabilities, which are maintained by a State that is the direct descendant of and heir to England's Dublin Castle rule in Ireland. Producers are charged too little for land and capital and too much for labour. It is necessary to change this pattern of costs so that producers pay more for land and capital and less for labour. That can easily and effectively be done by taxing the resources that are too cheap (land and capital/savings) and by de-taxing the resource that is too dear (labour). The cost of resources to producers can in this way be made to reflect their economic value rather than to reflect inherited colonial privilege.' (*A Radical's Response*)

Inherited colonial privilege had led to what Crotty called 'the paradox of property', namely, that the more expensive and costly land and property become, the more inefficiently they tend to be used. In Ireland this meant that if public policy measures were beneficial to the landed interest - landlords in the nineteenth century, owner-occupying farmers in the twentieth - they will be harmful to the non-landed interest. And if they are harmful to the landed interest they will be beneficial to the non-landed interest. His thinking on the land question echoed that of the nineteenth century political leaders, Michael Davitt and James Fintan

Lalor. The Land Acts of Davitt's day and later had replaced some 10,000 landlords by 500,000 or so owner-occupying farmers, of whom some 20,000 graziers owned half the land. Davitt had favoured the idea of a State landlord appropriating for the community by means of a land tax the rent or surplus to land which the tenants formerly paid to the private landlords. Instead of land use stagnating under absolute private ownership, as has occurred widely in modern Ireland, production from land should in principle be maximised under a system of revenue-maximising land taxes, just as it had previously been under a regime of competitive rents.

Professor Joe Lee has called *Irish Agricultural Production* 'a monument of the Irish intellect'. It is historical revisionism of the best kind, illuminating many matters hitherto obscure. Despite the focus of its title, its subject is the general economic history of Ireland since the seventeenth century. The book has had a seminal influence on the study of 19th century Irish economic history. It is scarcely an exaggeration to say that much of the large volume of academic work that has been done on the nineteenth century Irish land system since its publication - by scholars such as Solow, Donnelly, Vaughan, Bew, Mokyr and Ó Gráda - consists largely of metaphorical footnotes to Crotty's work, agreeing with him, arguing with him or developing his insights.

Crotty's view coincided with that of the revolutionary nationalist and trade union leader James Connolly, advanced in his book *Labour in Irish History,* that the prosperity of late eighteenth-century Ireland and its accompanying population expansion were less due to the influence of the semi-autonomous Grattan's Parliament of the time than to the high demand for grain in Britain in the years of the early Industrial Revolution, when the combination of the Corn Laws and the French Wars kept out cheaper continental grain. In those days the mass of Irish people fed themselves on potatoes, paid the landlord's rent in corn and typically fed a pig or two on the leftover potato scraps. Crotty showed how Irish exports of corn and bacon were closely correlated in the period. The high demand for labour in a potato and corn-growing economy enabled people to marry young and underlay the huge population expansion of late eighteentth and early nineteenth century Ireland.

Irish Agricultural Production charts the changes in the relative prices of grain and beef during the nineteenth century. The rise in meat prices compared to grain prices underpinned the decline in the demand for farm labour in Ireland, and the consequent falling marriage rate, the rise in the average age at marriage, the high rate of celibacy and high rate of net emigration that occurred in that century and continued into this. These trends underlay the fall in the island's population from 8.5 million in the 1840s to 4.3 million in the early 1960s. Crotty shows that the shift from labour-intensive corn growing to land-intensive cattle production, which was popularly summed up in the old phrase 'the land for the bullock and the people for the road', dated back to the end of the Napoleonic Wars. It antedated the Great Irish Famine of the 1840s, which was therefore not the economic watershed that had previously been claimed, although it gave impetus to existing trends. As regards the Great Famine itself, Crotty concluded that it 'might have been prevented by a revolution in the tenure system and never, as has been suggested, by the mere reform of it.'

In a later study of the Irish economy, *Ireland in Crisis, A Study of Capitalist Colonial Undevelopment* (1986) Crotty elaborates on what he calls the 'success stories' of nineteenth century Ireland, a society which he regarded as a fundamentally unhealthy one, whose problems were rooted in private ownership of land. The first success story was the

Banks, which channelled the surplus of land rents and savings out of the country to help the industrialisation of Britain. The second was the Catholic Church, which experienced a huge increase in recruitment to male and female religious orders and to foreign missionary activity, as well as a boom in church building, at this time. These trends were underpinned by the contemporary low marriage rate, which in turn arose from the lack of access to land for many of the children of the farming class in an increasingly pastoral rural economy. The third success story was Messrs Guinness and the network of public houses that spread over the country as people sought to drown their sorrows in alcohol. And the fourth was the industrialization of North-East Ireland. This had its roots in the 'Ulster custom' of the eighteenth century, which gave the mainly Protestant Ulster tenants less easy access to land than their counterparts in the South, but more security when they did gain access. That in turn encouraged capital formation among rural flax-growers, fostered linen manufacture and laid the basis of Belfast's nineteenth century engineering industry. There Catholic-Protesant enmity in turn facilitated employer-worker solidarity and made the Harland and Wolfe shipyard into 'a monument to Protestant-Catholic antipathy in Ireland.'

Following the publication of *Irish Agricultural Production* Crotty sold his farm in Kilkenny in an unworldly gesture that was, however, typical of the man.

> I would have escaped sooner from the burden of land ownership, but to have done so would have exposed me to the charge of first selling land and then proposing to tax its value away. Offering it to the Land Commission at their valuation, following publication of my book, appeared to be the least culpable way of disposing of a disagreeable responsibility. It would of course have been possible and profitable to have retained the land and to

have continued to draw the conacre rent. ... For my part, I
was unsure of being able to conduct a sustained attack on
property in Irish land if I continued to profit from that institution. (*A Radical's Response*)

For a period he acted as economic adviser to the Irish
Creamery Milk Suppliers Association, which organised the
dairy farmers of the province of Munster. For them he
developed the concept of the two-tier milk price, whereby
the Government through the creameries subsidised the offer
of a higher price for a farmer's first few thousand gallons of
milk than for production over that amount, with the rate of
subsidy gradually tapering off as output rose. This scheme
was implemented by Fianna Fáil Agricultural Minister Neil
Blaney. It was a policy obviously beneficial to the interests
of smaller producers and lasted until Ireland joined the EEC
in 1973. Today similar measures are being considered by
Brussels in an attempt to limit the cost of its Common
Agricultural Policy and orient support towards the more
numerous small farm producers and away from the large
ones who have been the principal beneficiaries of the
Common Agricultural Policy over the years.

In the 1960s the Third World development 'industry'
was in full spate. Crotty's unusual background of practical
farming experience and academic economics training made
him ideally fitted to take advantage of it. He resigned his
university lectureship and for a decade worked as an
economic consultant with the World Bank and various
governments in a score of countries across South East Asia,
India, Africa and Latin America. Here, as in Ireland, he
championed economic policies that would benefit the mass
of small agriculturists rather than a minority of big ones.

The Lactose Intolerance Theory of Civilisation

The intellectual stimulus of his Third World experience enabled Crotty to pioneer a new field in comparative economics.

> It became quickly apparent in the Third World that here was a very extensive yet largely untouched field of study that could reveal much about the human condition. Though normally dwarfed in terms of value of output by cropping, livestock worldwide occupied twice as much land as crops; and whereas any one crop, such as wheat or rice, was grown by only a proportion of cropgrowers on a small proportion of the world's total cropland, the keeping of cattle and buffaloes was practised universally and by more people than any other enterprise - yet there had to date been no systematic study of the economics of the world's cattle and buffalo keeping. (*A Radical's Response*)

The result was his book *Cattle, Economics and Development*, published in 1980 by the Commonwealth Agricultural Bureau. A hugely ambitious study of the interaction of cattle production, social mores, land use and property ownership across the five continents, this is a markedly original contribution to development economics. In some societies cattle are valued for their meat, in others for their milk and calves, in some as draught animals, in others for their dung, in some they are privately owned, in others they are grazed communally. This gives rise in different societies to different value ratios for cows, calves, fodder, land and labour, whose interaction Crotty examines in a work that throws a flood of light on the causes of development and 'undevelopment' in different parts of the world.

In India he discovered something that was not in any of the textbooks he had read, yet is supremely important in the world's cattle economy. The world's cows come in two

sorts, the result of millenia of genetic evolution: those of the
First World, which are of the *Bos taurus* type, that let down
their milk with or without the presence of their live calves;
while the cows of Africa and most of Asia are of the *Bos
indicus* type, that lactate only in the presence of their live
calves. He concluded that the deification of the cow by
Hinduism and the consequent tabooing of the slaughter and
consumption of cattle was a brilliant social innovation which
gave India an abundance of draught animals. That abundance enables India to produce more food from its land
surface than is produced from any comparable area of land
in the world. The deification of the cow prevented India's
land resources, subsequent to their conquest by the Northern
pastoralist invaders, from being diverted, like those of
Northern Eurasia, into milk and beef production for a small
pastoral population, and that country from being transformed
into a sparsely populated cattle walk. Something of this sort
did occur in Africa, however, where cattle are used
overwhelmingly for milk and meat rather than draught and
where, on almost eight times as much land, only a little more
than half as many people are supported, at a generally lower
level of nutrition, as on the sub-continent of India, Pakistan
and Bangladesh.

Probably the most original and interesting part of this
book is Crotty's preliminary outline of what is likely to
become known as the lactose intolerance theory of the
origins of European civilisation, or of 'capitalism', as Crotty
called it. He uses the word 'capitalism' in a special sense to
refer to the accumulation of capital in the form of cattle,
seed, farm implements, winter-fodder and buildings in the
forest lands of North and Central Europe in the millenia
before Christ and the millenium after, long before the
modern capitalist 'industrial revolution'. He expanded on his

theory in a lengthy appendix, occupying nearly half the volume, of his 1986 book, *Ireland in Crisis.*

Because Crotty's later books mingled an examination of Ireland's economic problems with a theory of the origins of capitalism and modern civilisation, he tended to fall between two stools so far as appreciation of the originality of his economic discoveries was concerned. His Irish readers would not in general be interested in a theory of the origins of civilisation, while specialists in world history were unlikely to be particularly interested in Ireland. Dr Lars Mjoset, Research Director at the Norwegian Institute for Social Research, was the first economist writing on the Irish economy to take Crotty's work seriously, because Crotty's contemporaries among Irish economists in general tended to regard him as an iconoclast and maverick. Mjoset makes several favourable references to Crotty's work in his own comparative study of Ireland and other small, though more successful, European economies, *The Irish Economy in a Comparative Institutional Perspective* (1993). He advised Crotty to make his general theory rather than the local Irish variation of it the focus of his last book, which he was working on at the time of his death in 1994 and which is awaiting publication at the time of writing of this essay. As Mjoset said in a publisher's reader's report on a first draft of this work, which was passed on to Crotty for his consideration:

> Ray Crotty is one of Ireland's most distinguished social science scholars, perhaps even the most interesting one. … He has developed a very original theory within the field of "universal history", which addresses nothing less than the dynamics of ancient civilisations and of the uniqueness of Western European development. … His approach is so original that it should be exposed to reviews and comment by the international academic community

which works in this field. I am convinced that the book will receive great attention among students and scholars in this field if they just become aware of it.

Lactose intolerance is a device of nature to expedite weaning and to ensure that mothers, having fulfilled their role in feeding their offspring in infancy, are then set free to re-engage in their primary natural task of reproduction. Various peoples around the world are lactose intolerant or malabsorbent; that is, consuming milk after infancy makes them ill. Lactose tolerance is based on a genetic mutation acquired in ancient times by pastoralist peoples, the Northern Eurasians, the Bedouin and the Nilo-Hamites of Africa. Without it there would be no modern dairy industry. Today thousands of years of genetic evolution have resulted in high proportions of adult Africans, Europeans and Indians being able to consume milk - they are lactose tolerant. On the other hand, nearly all adult East and South East Asians and indigenous Americans have a repugnance to milk - they are lactose malabsorbent. In ancient times the acquisition of lactose tolerance made it possible for more pastoralists, and therefore more efficient pastoralists, to subsist on given pastoral resources. It shifted the ancient balance of power away from the crop-growing, lactose malabsorbent peoples who built the first city civilisations in the river valleys of the Tigris, Euphrates, Indus, Nile and Yangtze, towards the pastoralists. The modern world is one created by the Indo-European pastoralist peoples who, having acquired lactose tolerance, domesticated the horse and discovered metallurgy. Their acquisition of lactose tolerance was the basis of their survival and increased living standards.

Crotty's outline of the origins of European civilisation shows the originality and sweep of his historical vision:

What was new was the scale on which the pastoralists of Western Europe used their cattle to grow crops. In a location where the net return for the seed planted was only one-third as much as on the Mediterranean littoral and only one-ninth as much as in Egypt, the only way to grow the crops that were essential for the survival of cattle was to use large numbers of cattle to cultivate extensive areas of cleared land to grow sufficient low-yielding crops to fodder the cattle through the winter and to feed the crop-growers through most of the year. ... The pastoralists who entered the Central Western Europe forest some 5,000 years ago, in order to secure a given output, had to use vastly more resources that had been saved from consumption than other producers. That is to say, they had to use far more capital. This greatly increased capital/output ratio was capitalist production. ... People for the first time ever, four or five thousand years ago, found in the forests of Central Western Europe the opportunity, by their own efforts and not through enslaving others, to escape from the tyranies of want, ignorance, custom and of arbitrary absolute governments. ... Uniquely there capital became the key to production. Production in all other societies was determined by the fixed amount of land or slaves available. But neither the amount nor the productivity of capital was inherently limited. (*Ireland in Crisis*)

Individualist Capitalist Colonialism

Capitalism, so defined, gave rise in turn to individualism and the rule of law. The latter was the expression of the unique political-economic relationship that existed between the individual and society in a situation where land did not limit production and where the individual's production sustained himself and simultaneously enhanced the productivity and security of his fellows. The individual hunter-gatherer, the individual on the communally grazed rather than individually owned pastures and in the crowded river valleys of ancient society, were powerless to add to production by their own efforts. Rather, by their presence they reduced the amount available to all the other members of society. Echoing Marx, Crotty saw the principal concern of law as the protection of the property that has been the economic basis of law-governed societies.

Crotty's study of the Third World brought home to him that Ireland's serious economic problems had analogies in most former colonies of the European capitalist powers. Here societies organised in communal, non-individualistic ways - as Ireland was in the days of the clans and Brehon law - had an alien system imposed on them which conflicted profoundly with their traditional way of doing things. Their indigenous social structures had been ruptured by the externally imposed institutions of 'individualistic capitalism', in particular private property in livestock and pasture land, condemning them to permanent 'undevelopment'. Development he defined as occurring where a society has (a) more people who were better off, and (b) fewer people who were as badly off, as at a previous time. The first condition is quite commonly fulfilled in the present-day Third World, but not the second. By these criteria some 140 States that were former colonies of the individualist capitalist European powers, comprising some three billion people and half the globe's inhabitants, have found themselves consistently 'undeveloping' rather than developing in the modern period. These States are nowadays politically independent, as local élites have succeeded in indigenizing colonial privilege. They included Ireland, Europe's only capitalist colony, but they contrast with two kinds of society that either benefited from capitalist colonialism or else escaped colonisation. The first of these comprised the settler colonies of North America and Australasia, where the indigenous inhabitants were either insignificant in number or were exterminated by the white colonists from Europe. The second group comprised the East Asian cultures of China, Japan and the Pacific Rim, as well as Russia, which largely escaped individualist capitalist colonisation and borrowed eclectically from the West, taking what suited them, while keeping their own cultures. The East Asian countries have rapidly developed in recent decades and are characterised by forms of collectivist psychology, behaviour and institutions which Crotty was one of the first to draw attention to. Ireland differed from the former capitalist colonies only in that people have been able to escape from it by emigrating. This has been the fate of nearly half of those born and surviving beyond infancy in Ireland since the mid-nineteenth century, whereas people are effectively imprisoned in most Third World countries and prevented from emigrating. Crotty was pessimistic about the ability of the countries colonised by individualistic capitalism to overcome the effects of the trauma of colonialism, although he hoped that Ireland perhaps might set an example.

Naturally Crotty's advocacy of land taxation did not make him popular with the powerful Irish farmer interest, in particular the large-farmer dominated Irish Farmers Association. They disliked him particularly when in 1972 he opposed Irish membership of the European Economic Community. He saw the EEC as aggravating the historical problems of Irish agriculture, increasing land values and cosseting the landed interest. His denial that higher EEC food prices under the CAP would revolutionise Irish agricultural output - for which he was contemptuously scoffed at during the referendum debate on Irish membership of the EEC - has been largely borne out by events. Net output in Irish agriculture scarcely changed in the first decade of Irish membership. Crotty emphasised that higher EEC food prices, while benefiting farmers, would raise labour and living costs. In the 1980s and 1990s a borrowing spree by Irish Governments to subsidise private capital investment and expand unproductive public employment led to heavy increases in taxation, which made employing people more expensive, on top of the higher labour costs caused by the CAP, and helped destroy much of indigenous Irish industry. Criticising the economic policies of T K Whitaker and Garret FitzGerald, Crotty wrote:

> The ultimate consequence of the Whitakerian-Geraldine policy of reintegrating Ireland's former capitalist colonial economy with the economies of the metropolitan capitalist countries has been to intensify Irish economic dependence. It has given rise to a high cost agriculture that produces with little reference to consumers' needs. ... Indigenous Irish manufacturing industry has been eclipsed. ... New manufacturing jobs now come almost exclusively from foreign firms. Irish dependence on the metropolitan capitalist economy is clinched by its large and rapidly expanding national debt, which is the inescapable consequence of fostering exports through government deficit financing, which has been the nub of Whitakerian-Geraldine policy. Ireland is now so dependent on foreign borrowing that the entire economy would collapse overnight and the polity would disintegrate if foreign credits ceased to be available. Ireland's metropolitan dependence, with respect to agricultural prices, jobs and credit is now far more complete than that of any other former capitalist colony. (*Ireland.in Crisis*)

The Single European Act

In 1987 Raymond Crotty became known internationally for his landmark constitutional action in the Supreme Court on the Single European Act. The Government purported to ratify this European Treaty by majority vote in parliament. Crotty contended that the transfer of sovereignty to the

European Communities entailed by the SEA could only be done by referendum of the Irish people themselves. In December 1986 he sought and won an injunction in the High Court restraining the State from ratifying the Treaty until this issue was tried. Following a lengthy constitutional action in the High Court and Supreme Court, the latter found in Crotty's favour. As he said at the time, 'The courts have caught the politicians with their hands in the till of the people's rights.' This delayed by six months the coming into force of the SEA, to the annoyance of the Europhiles in Brussels and elsewhere, as all the other EEC States had already ratified the treaty, which however required unanimity before it could come into force. Following the Supreme Court's verdict it would have been open to the Government to have insisted to its fellow EEC members that the Single European Act Treaty should be altered to take account of its unconstitutionality in Ireland. Indeed if a general election had not supervened between the High Court and Supreme Court stages of Crotty's legal action, this might well have happened. Instead, the new Fianna Fáil Government, led by Charles Haughey, pushed through a constitutional change by referendum to permit the ratification of the SEA, using large sums of taxpayers' money to advocate a 'yes' vote in newspaper and billboard advertising, as had never previously been done in Irish referenda. Eight years later, after Crotty's death, such one-sided use of public money in referenda was in turn judged unconstitutional by the Supreme Court in the McKenna case.

Crotty - 'Citizen Crotty' as he was called in sections of the Irish media - had put his reputation and personal finances in jeopardy by taking his court action, but he got small thanks for it. He had, however, established the important principle that increases in the powers of the European institutions required a popular referendum. A lone individual had asserted the rights of the citizen against the State and the whole of Europe. One issue in the Crotty case had been the plaintiff's *locus standi*. Could Mr Crotty show that he would himself be injured personally if the Government ratified the SEA Treaty in the manner it wanted to? Referring to the flood of European laws that would pour forth from Brussels if the SEA got though, Supreme Court Justice Brian Walsh aptly commented to the court, 'Mr Crotty's *locus standi* is that of someone standing with his finger in the dyke!'

A strong individualist, Raymond Crotty fitted neither the conventional left-wing nor right-wing mould. Naturally iconoclastic, his outspoken criticisms of official economic policy did not endear him to Ireland's economics establishment, among whose conventionally minded and politically timorous ranks intellectual boat-rocking is rare. As far as can be ascertained, his pioneering work *Cattle, Economics and Development* was not reviewed in a single Irish journal, although it attracted and continues to attract significant attention abroad. Crotty was not made welcome in the economics Departments of the Irish universities, and he in turn did not bother to conceal his contempt for mainstream Irish economics and what he regarded as its virtually unparalleled record of presiding over and rationalising social disaster in the country. In contrast to Ireland's economists, its academic historians and statisticians have been more welcoming of his work. The combination of Crotty's intellectual isolation vis-à-vis the Irish economics profession, the unconventional way he had himself come to economics and the urgency of his personal concern to win support for his prescriptions for Ireland's traditional emigration and unemployment problems, often led him to express his views in extreme or exaggerated form, especially in his popular journalism. This militated further against their being sympathetically understood by his Irish contemporaries.

The intellectual case for land taxation seemed so clear to Crotty that sometimes he gave the impression of thinking that force of argument alone would suffice to convert people to his views, underestimating the weight of the powerful interests that stood to lose by any such measure. There is, however, now widespread acceptance in the Irish social science community of the validity of Crotty's basic contention that the heart of Ireland's jobless problem is that of the employment of labour being dear, in large part because the use of land and capital is cheap.

Outside Ireland there is growing awareness among economists, economic historians and 'world system' theorists of the significance of Raymond Crotty's discoveries in pastoral economics for understanding the genesis of capitalism and European civilisation. It is well known that capital formation in agriculture was crucial in Europe's early economic take-off, as it has been more recently for the developing East Asian economies. On the other hand, the low level of capital formation in agriculture seems to have been crucial for the 'undevelopment' of the African ones. Raymond Crotty's theory of lactose intolerance has made a unique contribution to economics and economic history by showing the special role of cattle and the use of pasture land in the accumulation of capital in agriculture. Whether agriculture development is of such significance in the later stages of industrialisation, when modern technologies may in principle be availed of by all societies, is for specialists in economic development to consider. In doing so, however, they are bound to be in intellectual debt to a thinker whom economic history will surely recognise as the most original social scientist to come out of modern Ireland. †

Books and Pamplets by Raymond Crotty

Irish Agriculture and the European Economic Community, 1962, Limerick, Ireland, Irish Creamery Milk Suppliers Association, 52 pp.

Irish Agricultural Production, Its Volume and Structure, 1966, Cork, Ireland, University Press, 384 pp.

Irish Agriculture and the Common Market, 1972, Dublin, Common Market Study Group, 25 pp.

The Cattle Crisis and the Small Farmer, 1974, Dundalk, Ireland, The National Land League, 59 pp.

Cattle, Economics and Development, 1980, Slough, England, Commonwealth Agricultural Bureau, 253 pp.

The Irish Land Question and Sectarianism, 1981, Ilford, England, Economic and Social Research Association, 15 pp.

Ireland in Crisis, A Study in Capitalist Colonial Undevelopment, 1986, Dingle, Ireland, Brandon Press, 296 pp.

A Radical's Response, 1988, Dublin, Poolbeg Press, 170 pp.

Japan and Ireland, a Comparative Study, 1991, Tokyo, Institute of Comparative Economic Studies, Hosei University, 38 pp.

Farming Collapse, National Opportunity, 1992, Dublin, Amárach-Ireland 2000, 91 pp.

Maastricht, Time to Say No!, 1992, Dublin, The National Platform for Employment, Democracy, Neutrality, 44 pp.

---

† This essay is based on a paper given to the Desmond Greaves Summer School in 1994.

6. THE NORTH: A CONUNDRUM OF IDENTITY

JACK BENNETT

The vexed question of the identity of the Protestants of Ulster calls for a little more down-to-earth common sense and for much less of that imaginative speculation heard in recent times from the dreamy groves of Academe - not to mention other more dubious sources. Now that we have entered the arena of political debate, as a result of the peace process, the fog of confusion over imagined 'identities' needs to be dispersed if the cause of reconciliation is to be pursued seriously and with intellectual integrity.

Simply to pose the question invites the answer. Are the Protestant people and the Catholic people really all that different? Do those people whose religion is of some Protestant variety - if they have any religion at all - also possess other recognisably different characteristics that set them distinctly apart from 'the other sort' as they walk the streets of Belfast or the by-ways of rural Ulster? Do the different religions pursue radically different life-styles in their day-to-day activities? Is there anything that can sensibly be argued to mark them out as belonging, as some would claim, to two different 'cultures'? They go, it's true, in different directions to church of a Sunday - if they go at all. And that is about all it amounts to.

The burden of this essay is to argue what most people in Northern Ireland, Catholic and Protestant, already know full well - that the Protestant people do not have any particularly different identity that can be defined in objective sociological or any other scientific terms. Despite all the recent efforts to fit them out with one, they have no social identity apart from that they share with the other people around them - that is, their Catholic neighbours. They all speak the same language - a version of English with some Elizabethan survivals that stamps them all as 'Paddies' to the average English person. They speak it in identical accents which vary only from region to region. What we have is a community that shares very similar and recognisably common characteristics. It also shares very much in common, something peculiar to itself - something that few people elsewhere want to know about. That is a propensity to celebrate its religious differences. The British - whose name is so often invoked to sustain that quarrel - regard it as something exceptionally and exasperatingly 'Irish'. So, in their very differences, the different 'religious' sectors have something that could, in a sense, be said to unite them and invest them with an essentially common identity. There we have the paradox which any analysis of the problem must address.

The fault of some of the academic contribution to the debate in recent times is that it has been, indeed, academic - a sort of playfield for exercising those witty talents cultivated in student debating societies and to allow a few university teachers to show how clever they are. Their efforts have produced little but theoretical fantasies - some of them palpably fatuous, as we shall see, and some laborious excursions into the realms of contrived ingenuity. Attempts have been made to manufacture, or to invent, radically divergent features to separate the religious groups into two irreconcilable peoples, or tribes. Various theses have been proffered which, in effect, serve only to uphold Protestant sectarianism as a sort of natural outcrop of Irish history.

Indubitably, we may say that politics in the closed-in and restricted Northern Ireland context present us with an unusual and deep-seated sectarian problem. We have, as a result, a situation recognisably abnormal in which, indeed, normal politics can hardly be said to prevail at all. It must also be observed that the predominating and causative factor in this sectarian scene is the problem of Orange-Unionist-Loyalism which has, to some extent among sections of the population, hijacked the consciousness of being Protestant (although by no means everywhere or entirely), and which could be described as political Protestantism. To say so can hardly be held to be excessively controversial.

Few would deny that the six-county political unit was originally carved out as an Orange unionist enclave, and formed into 'a Protestant state for a Protestant people'. So it is not surprising that it should retain that intrinsically sectarian character with which it was stamped at its genesis. For the greater part of its existence, indeed, unionist politicians thought it in no way reprehensible to make frank and unashamed appeals to political Protestantism. Some of them did not refrain from indulging in a fierce anti-Catholic bigotry.

However, there came a time when it was perceived that overt sectarianism was frowned upon, especially in Britain. This gave rise to the need to disguise in a new dress the underlying sectarian ingredient of unionist politics, and this in turn gave rise to a remarkable variety of fantasy theories. A unionist politician has told us that the two religions constitute two races. More fanciful sophistry has tried to argue that they are two nations. Cognate to these notions is the assertion heard of late that the Protestants are not Irish at all. Way-out versions hold that the Ulster Protestants are the ancient Cruthin who went to Scotland, became the Picts, and came back to claim their territory after the Reformation. Less strident and more cautious voices - aware no doubt of the danger of appearing too ridiculous - advance the idea that the Protestant population has simply some set of naturally different traditions or just a different culture, not to mention things like 'heritage' and even 'birthright'. Two cultures, two nations, two this or two that - any two damn anything will do to separate the sheep from the goats and to rationalise what is, plainly and simply, an irrational religious divide.

None of these notions can stand up to any critical scrutiny, as we shall see, but it should be obvious to begin with that some of the divisive theories we have been hearing from a few academics are the last thing we need if our aim is reconciliation, and if we are to escape from the intolerable and stifling straitjacket of sectarianism. It may be interesting to note at once, however, that the idea that Protestants are not Irish, or not 'really Irish', while associated today with a minority of loyalist sectarian groups, was never part of the broader unionist tradition. In the past, it was associated more with the outlook of a certain type of Catholic sectarian nationalism, which used to be familiar as a 'Hibernian' Catholic mentality.

It is tempting, therefore, to suspect that the outlook and opinions expressed by a few academics and writers such as Conor Cruise O'Brien, who appear to consider tribal and religious enmity a natural condition of the human species, may be the products, perhaps, of an ingrained sectarian mind-set subconsciously acquired from a background influenced by Hibernian-type Catholic nationalism. O'Brien has occasionally dropped a remark that suggests he views Protestants who take a nationalistic position as eccentrics or mavericks. That view could be taken as conforming with a doctrine of the naturalness of loyalist-sectarian bigotry and a belief that sectarian conflict is only to be expected, together with all O'Brien's other favourite bloodbath scenarios.

Now, whether Ireland should be united or not, or whether it should have a government of its own or not - those are political questions. And political opinions are not genetically inherited. Yet that very insistence is implicit in much of the theorising of the sectarian two-nation tribalist advocates. Certainly, political opinions are often passed on in families, but it is not unknown for young people to differ from their parents, as we know - not to mention their grandparents. It is to the ability of people to change their political views that we must look today for any sort of hopeful change that will move us forward to a new political solution of our problems.

In considering the Irish identity of the Protestant people, it should be unnecessary to stress that most Protestant people in Ulster - indeed, you could say all of them up until recent times - have always been conscious of sharing a sense of Irishness with their Catholic fellow countrymen and women. It is a relatively new thing among them to be anti-Irish as such, and even today attitudes of that sort are found only in a few ghetto areas where ignorance flourishes and where the broader horizons of reality are obscured by the backyard walls. To illustrate the point, we'll take a quote or two from a very timely book published recently in Belfast - *Thomas Carnduff: Life and Writings*. Tom Carnduff, who died in 1956, was very much in the Protestant tradition. From the Sandy Row, and active in the Independent Orange Order when it was a politically radical institution, he was a working man, a poet, playwright and writer. Of his Irishness, he wrote:

> The fact that five generations of my family were connected with Orangeism, and I myself have been Worshipful Master of an Independent Orange lodge, does not make me any less of an Irishman ... My earliest recollection of what my feelings were towards my native land was an intense pride in being born an Irishman ... The six counties still remain a cultural part of the Irish nation ... I am not one of those people who believe that Ireland will

remain a sliced-up country for all time. No artificial bor-
der can split a nation in two by merely drawing a line of
demarcation ... Time can heal all the sores and tribulations
of a disrupted people ... Belfast is an Irish city ... The
Protestants of Belfast are as Irish as the Catholics ... The
country has a minority problem, which is religious not racial in character, however much British interference in the
matter has made it an issue between the two countries.

It has been asked, as a rhetorical question implying a
negative response, whether a group of people can be
considered Irish if they themselves do not think they are - or,
to use the scholastic phrase favoured by obfuscators, if they
'do not perceive themselves to be.' It is a trick question. It
assumes the 'perception' to be prevalent, which it is not, and
it ignores the fact that it is held only by those wishing to
promote and exacerbate, intentionally or otherwise, sectarian divisions. The answer, therefore, must be: the
Protestants are Irish, whether or not they think they are, or
whether or not they perceive themselves to be such.

People get stamped with the indelible characteristics of
their own people and nation - whether they like it or not - by
the unavoidable experience of being born and growing up
among other people much like themselves. The characteristics they acquire are recognised, objectively from outside, by
other peoples. Cruise O'Brien, whose opinions I seldom
share, once said something very wise about Irishness to the
effect that being Irish was a matter of being involved in and
being moulded by Irish affairs. It is a definition that could
perhaps be said to give Orangemen a status almost 'more
Irish than Irish'. That people can sometimes 'perceive'
themselves to be something other than what they really are is
not an altogether unknown form of delusion. It has been seen
elsewhere. At one time a considerable proportion of the
German people perceived themselves as herrenvolk, and

other peoples as untermenschen. Many strange beliefs are encountered in racialist and sectarian myth.

How about the 'two cultures'? Again, any search for a definably different culture for the Protestant people of the North must prove equally unfruitful - whether we take the word in its broader anthropological sense or in the narrower sense of producing distinctive cultural works in, say, literature, poetry, music and so on. The subject was examined in an address to the British Association in Bristol in 1986 by Dr Anthony Buckley, speaking as assistant keeper of anthropology at the Ulster Folk Museum. He said: 'The distinctiveness of Protestant and Catholic cultural forms is often quite minimal. There has long been in the expression of political and religious differences a great deal of borrowing, to the extent that any attempt to project present-day symbolism into the past and call them "distinctive traditions" is almost impossible.'

Further: 'Emblems and activities, widely recognised to be specifically factional, not only have aspects derived from an inherently common culture, but they are used for purposes which are found on "both sides" in Northern Ireland.' He also said it was 'misleading to argue that there are two traditions' in Ulster - i.e. the Catholic and nationalist and Protestant unionist traditions.

If an ethnographic approach was used to examine what were regarded as 'traditions' in Ireland, he said, it could be seen that the culture of Ireland in general and Ulster in particular was made up of elements both diverse and uniform. 'Many supposedly sectarian differences are better seen as either regional variations or as variations between social classes.' 'Such differences have been popularly translated into sectarian or political terms in a manner which does not correspond to the facts.' He based much of his study on the different groups of English dialect spoken in

Ireland, and stated: 'There are no distinctly Protestant or Catholic dialects, nor agricultural practices or pottery techniques, nor styles for cooking. Family life is much the same on both sides, as indeed is the broader social morality. In general, then, we may say not that there exists a Catholic and a Protestant culture in Ireland, but rather that there are cultural differences which coincide with both regional and class distinctions.'

Here we have the evidence of an expert witness. We all share 'an inherently common culture'. We may certainly take his word for it. In saying so, he was saying what most sensible people in Northern Ireland already know full well.

That being the case, it is hardly surprising that no evidence of a distinctly Protestant culture in the field of the arts can be found. Politically speaking, we must insist that there is no such thing as a unionist 'culture', for political unionism tends rather to be anti-culture, since it thrives on ignorance. Most of the best Protestant writers and poets - both recent and not so recent - were national or nationalist in their outlook. Few, if any, were unionist in the modern understanding of the term. Even Samuel Ferguson could not be counted among the ideologists of modern unionism.

In a perceptive article on that aspect of the theme in the *Guardian* newspaper, the Belfast writer and novelist, Ronan Bennett, made some incisive observations - and I quote: 'The Protestant North has produced art, but rarely is it art that celebrates the world that spawned it. More often it is an angry reaction to the prevalence of bigotry, claustrophobia and paranoia.' Further: 'Most artists and writers who have emerged from Ulster Protestantism have tended to move away - physically and mentally - from the world that bred them. To remain is to be enclosed in a world where "culture" is restricted to little more than flute bands, Orange marches and the chanting of sectarian slogans at football matches.'

One artist he spoke to, describing 'an atmosphere of suffocation', said: 'It is an intolerable mental world to have to inhabit.' We have an echo here again of the thoughts of Tom Carnduff, quoted earlier.

On cultural matters, Carnduff in his day also noted that 'the mind is intimidated and confused' by sectarianism, and that, for the writer, 'this intimidation of the mind enters into every sphere of cultural life. The artist is shut in too ... Writers who make their living in State or municipal employment have to be ever on guard over what they write ... there is a cultural problem in Ireland deriving from the sectarian problem.'

Yet rays of hope and reality break through at times. A choir from Methodist College in Belfast won first place in a contest in England not so long ago with 'She moves through the Fair'. Their Irish cultural heritage stood by them. Obviously they cannot have considered that heritage to be in any way 'foreign' or 'alien' to some different Protestant cultural identity. Certain sectarian Orange elements, however, now insist that all things Irish are indeed foreign to their own 'tradition'. But if we were to ask them, for instance, how Percy French could be slotted into their blinkered scheme of things, what could they say? The 'Mountains of Mourne', 'Ballyjamesduff', the 'West Clare Railway'? Are those songs foreign to the Protestant community? The idea is absurd - just as all notions of a separate Protestant cultural identity are clearly absurd.

Where, then, does that leave us with the notion of 'two nations'? Two nations call for a great many more identifiable differences than we can so far perceive.

The truth is that the two nations 'theory', like all the rest of the theories promoted to magnify religious differences and give them some innate substance, cannot survive any close examination. There is no definition of a nation that could possibly be held to grant nationhood status to the northern Protestants. A strange nation, indeed, which never had a national liberation hero of its own, which never fought for self-determination and independence, which never produced a democratic national movement, but which aligned itself behind every anti-democratic imperialist cause in recent history.

An exercise in sophistry which attempted to grant some plausibility to the two nations notion was published a number of years ago by a geography teacher at Maynooth, D G Pringle, entitled, *One Island - Two Nations?* The query mark in the title was superfluous. Presenting himself as a sort of scholastic 'Marxist', he drew heavily on pseudo-Marxist ideas and quasi-Marxist jargon, which he then merged with the ideological propaganda of modern trans-national financial and industrial capitalism - which no longer needs, or wants, too many national states, and which therefore favours the now fashionable view that nationalism is out-dated. It is interesting to note that 'old hat nationalism based on outworn myths' is now one of those ready-made political opinions which can be bought off the hook and retailed parrot-like by every hack newspaper writer and politically illiterate unionist. Pringle made much of the schematics of Ernest Gellner. His tortured logic landed him in some curious contradictions, which were thoroughly dissected and demolished at the time in the *Irish Democrat* †.

A resolution passed by the unionist group in Belfast City Hall in February 1994 proclaimed the belief that 'the island of Ireland contains two nations'. It is an opinion, we see, that fits in comfortably with Orange prejudices. We may safely recognise it as just another way of expressing sectarian

---

† October, November and December, 1986.

sentiments. What two nations are they? Even if they really existed, they are so inextricably intermixed upon our common territory that there could be no reason to prevent them from getting together in, say, a federation to rule their own island for their own good. Unfortunately, the unionist mindset cannot grasp that sort of logic. All they have is their anti-Catholicism.

Perhaps the most fatuous flight of fantasy of all is that which describes the Protestants as 'British Ulster' and the Catholics as 'Irish Ulster' - a formulation again originating at a Hibernian-Catholic source but very quickly adapted to unionist political purposes. There is no such thing as a British nationality as such. There are three nationalities in Britain. The English may describe themselves as British. So can the Scots and the Welsh. What sort of British are Ulster Protestants? Just 'British British'? The one and only?

Being British is a political category which grants a citizenship to people who are British subjects. The people of Kenya and Cyprus, and elsewhere, were British until their political status changed, and the people of Northern Ireland may continue to be, or cease to be, British by decision of the Westminster parliament. There appears to be a subconscious awareness of that fact in unionist phraseology which insists that the Protestant people 'wish to remain' or are 'determined to remain' British. Whether or not the people of Britain consider them to be intrinsically British is another question - and it is a dubious one, as recent comments in even the most conservative British newspapers make quite clear.

Nevertheless, an academic at Queen's University, Liam Kennedy, produced a pamphlet a while back entitled *Two Ulsters - a Case for Repartition* in which he proceeds from the notion that there exist two distinct and irreconcilable tribes, one known as 'British Ulster' and the other as 'Irish

Ulster'. We may just possibly detect here another expression of an ingrained sectarian mind-set deriving from Hibernian Catholic nationalism. His work was an extravagant and ridiculous blueprint for an elaborate division of the six counties into a patchwork quilt of separate communities based on a sort of religious apartheid, some of which would belong to Britain and some to an Irish state. Using facile international parallels, he saw the example of the road from west Germany through east Germany - before unification - as a useful model, and suggested a similar road from the 'Irish' territory around Newry, running through 'British' territory to an 'Irish' enclave in west Belfast.

He makes a further argument for 'two nations' in Ireland out of the fact that two nation states exist on the one island of Hispaniola in the Caribbean - Haiti and the Dominican Republic - and that there are two nation states on the Iberian peninsula - Spain and Portugal. It is a hoary theme. It must have thrilled the hearts of every unionist sectarian apologist from the time it was first thought of. It is an obvious aunt sally.

The case for Irish self-determination in no way rests exclusively on geographical arguments. It is based on the reality that the people of Ireland share one common historical experience upon the ground of Ireland, and that their economic and political interests still coincide as a result. Their economic and political development and experience, as well as their interests and needs, differ in certain ways from those of the peoples of Britain. Our island borders help only to enhance the differences. The divergence of interests and needs as between Britain and Ireland - even if marginal as some might argue - is still such that it underlines our own shared identity in the economic field also. This is a point important to any realistic consideration of the practical questions of self-determination, as we shall see.

Liam Kennedy's pamphlet was 'borrowed' by the UDA and used as a pattern for a projected programme of ethnic cleansing and as a blueprint for driving the Catholic population out from extensive areas. The author, naturally, repudiated this appropriation of his ideas, but however ingenuous his motivation, his book nevertheless remains, in its effect, a mischievous and irresponsible exercise in magnifying religious differences and legitimising the sectarian mind-set.

Is there anything left that we can salvage to bestow a quality of distinctness on the Protestants of Ulster? What about the 'two traditions' we are told we all must have mutual respect and esteem for? We need to be careful here. If we are referring simply to different religious traditions, there should be no difficulty in accommodating them in reconciliation in any new changed framework that might be agreed. What must be recognised is that there exists no natural law, nor any established political principle, which insists that people of any particular religion must live under any particular flag or jurisdiction. To claim that Protestants can live only under the Union Jack - or even that only under it can they live 'comfortably' - is absurd, as well as being an obviously politico-sectarian tenet.

We may reasonably ask, therefore, under what sort of new political arrangements may we realistically expect the different religious denominations to live together in friendship. Can we expect them to do so within a political framework designed to keep them apart? It should be clear that the six-county political unit - still the greatest monument to religious sectarianism in Ireland - has had its day. It is on its way out. Whatever the direction or the pace of the change that is coming, there has to be a perceptible movement toward replacing it by something more conducive to the cause of reconciliation. A purely internal six-county settlement is now out of the question.

We must also recognise, of course, that there are also certain political traditions closely associated with the Protestant people - and with them only. Some of them are healthy traditions, and some of them deplorable. The mainstream Orange-unionist-loyalist tradition embraces the central notion of 'Kick the Pope and keep the Taigs in their place.' We can have no respect for that.

The ultra-reactionary nature of the Orange-unionist political movement throughout the last century, promoted by the gentry, the landlords, the magistrates and the aristocrats, survives in the obsequious grovelling of some Orange-loyalist elements towards their betters - symbolised on their banners with portraits of kings, queens, earls, dukes, captains of industry and other such idols of democracy. Devotion to imperialism is frankly portrayed as part of what they naïvely call their 'heritage' - in pictures, for example, of Queen Victoria handing a Bible to kneeling and subservient black toadies. This they call 'the secret of England's greatness' - a sentiment surely repulsive to most educated people today.

In the fight against landlordism, the Orange Order sided with the landlords, used its members as scabs to work on boycotted estates, and even employed some of them as thugs to terrorise tenants during the anti-tithe movement. This backward and reactionary character of mainstream Orangeism is attested not only by reputable historians like Hereward Senior, but also in official histories of the Orange Order itself, like that incredible collection in two volumes, attributed to R M Sibbett.

But perhaps some unionists might say today that it is simply 'British traditions' with which they feel an affinity, and with which they wish to remain associated. Difficulties arise here again. There are many different political traditions in Britain, some of them good and some of them bad. Political unionism has always been associated with the worst of them. Unionism inherits, in direct lineal descent, traditions personified in the tyrant Castlereagh. They can claim no kinship with Byron and Shelley, those English poets of the dawn of the democratic era, who execrated him as the man 'who cut his country's throat' (Ireland's), or who was likened to Murder, in 'a mask like Castlereagh'. Unionist politicians elected to Westminster were always among the most backward and reactionary MPs there. They voted consistently against every progressive measure, including the post-war welfare state. Throughout the previous century they opposed every bill for reform, every extension of the franchise, and every measure designed to ameliorate the conditions of working people.

On the other hand, the Irish movement for independence has always been broadly popular and truly democratic. From the United Irishmen onwards, the most advanced and radical elements in it had close relations with similar, radical, democratic and popular movements in Britain, such as the famous 'corresponding clubs'. The revolutionary Young Ireland movement and the Fenians were in close contact with the English Chartists, who were the forerunners of the modern British labour movement, and some Chartist leaders were former Fenians. Ex-Fenian Michael Davitt, who suffered dreadfully for his beliefs in English jails, was a working man who grew up in Lancashire and laboured in the mills there. He was the founder and editor of one of Britain's first Labour journals, the *Labour World*. In his later struggles to advance the well-being of the Irish peasantry he was assisted by the best spirits of English democracy - to name but one, the fine poet and anti-imperialist, Wilfred

Scawan Blunt, who was himself put in jail in Sligo in 1887 for his efforts on behalf of the Irish poor.

The Irish people share many good traditions, political and cultural, with the British peoples - an inevitable result of cross-cultural exchange - but it is only the Irish independence movement that today shares the best of British radical, popular and democratic traditions. Incidentally, it could be argued that more echoes can be heard of the cultural influence of Rabbie Burns in the Donegal Gaeltacht than can be found on the Shankill Road in Belfast. Another surprising and peculiar example of cross-cultural influence could be the extraordinary and fanatical support for Manchester United football club in Dublin and throughout the central and some western counties of Ireland.

If we are to look now for better political traditions among the Protestant people, there is no difficulty in finding much that deserves respect. Throughout the history of all Irish movements for independence, there has been a consistent, substantial and unbroken thread of support for the democratic cause among intelligent and thinking Protestants. In the last century, the Derry Protestant John Mitchel, of the Young Ireland movement, wrote an open letter to the Protestants of the North, for which offence he was sent as a felon convict to Van Diemen's land. He said: 'There is now no Protestant interest at all; there is absolutely nothing left for Protestant and Catholic to quarrel for: and if any man talks to you now of religious sects, when the matter in hand relates to civil and political rights, to administration of government, or distribution of property - depend upon it, though he wear a coronet on his head, he means to cheat you.' The Protestants, unfortunately, have been cheated for too long since.

Much later, during the Home Rule controversy, another famous Protestant spokesman emerged, the Presbyterian clergyman, the Rev J B Armour, who organised a rally of Protestants in Ballymony in favour of Home Rule in the face of the terror, intimidation and hysteria of the Carsonite anti-Catholic campaign. He denounced the Orange bigots as 'troglodytes' and described the day of the 'Ulster Covenant' as 'the Protestant fools' day'.

Who can ignore our own northern Protestant poet of those times, Alice Milligan, who died not so long ago, and who wrote some famous and enchanting rhymes in praise of the Fenians? Or another great Protestant nationalist, an Irishwoman of northern origin, Alice Stopford Green. She gave us a work of irreplaceable importance to Irish nationality - *The Making of Ireland and its Undoing*. She was the wife of a great English historian, J R Green, author of one of the best histories of England ever written, *A Short History of the English People*.

What can Orange-loyalist-unionism boast of in the way of traditions that can compare with all this? Here is where we must, indeed, take a cold look at that extraordinary, peculiar and exceptional phenomenon known as Ulster loyalism.

It may be considered a simplification - but one that is not so very far short of the mark - to say that it is this which constitutes the six-county problem. This is the problem that stands in the way of a reasonable solution of the political mess that is the six counties. Even now, at an advanced stage of the peace process, it is only too obvious that all unionist groups, including those some commentators in Dublin newspapers still like to call 'moderate', share certain common characteristics - all marked by an intransigence, an intolerance and a refusal to budge from the position that they will accept no settlement short of one based on the old cock o'the walk sectarian domination of one religion over the other. The most conservative of English newspapers are showing impatience with them. They are arriving at the point where they have no friends left in all the world and nobody wants them any more. It's about time they started to make friends with their own people who live around them.

Not a few scholarly works have been produced to analyse and explain the rise of this phenomenon. Some of them, like those of Peter Gibbon, are useful for the new insights and observations they offer, but many of them tend to simplify the origins of Orangeism as a natural and spontaneous thing - something which the British government had nothing to do with and could do nothing about. Historical facts, although thoroughly documented, are thus fudged. The reality is that Orangeism would not have survived into the nineteenth century, and could not have thrived for most of that century, but for the patronage of the imperial power, which recognised it as a useful instrument to keep the Irish divided. This is true in spite of those few periods when the movement was out of favour. Guns in thousands were sent to Orangemen throughout the country in 1797, before the great rebellion, and Lord Castlereagh was happy to provide them. Aristocrats gave their generous patronage to the Order, and it came to boast of having the royal Duke of Cumberland, brother of the king, as its Imperial Grand Master.

An American academic, David W Millar, in his book, *Queen's Rebels*, traces the origin of the modern unionist mentality to a medieval relationship of patron and client which assumed an implicit contract between the imperial power and colonial settlers. The survival of attitudes moulded by that concept - some centuries after the social relations upon which they were based have long passed away - stamps them as a sociological fossil. Their survival is reflected in the constant accusations of 'betrayal' levelled at the British government by Ian Paisley. There can be no such thing as betrayal if there is no contract, implicit or explicit, to grant some sort of favoured position to Protestants as such. Echoes of the same concept could also possibly be said to be heard in the familiar unionist-loyalist plaint about their service to Britain in two world wars - implying the existence of a reciprocal obligation and oblivious of the contribution from Redmondite nationalist Ireland. It would help to hasten the final and overdue demise of those notions if a British government were to make it clear that it no longer supported one side in the six county political arena - the Orange, loyalist side.

An unavoidable concomitant of the belief in a special status for Protestants - based on the 'contract' idea and inherited from centuries of English rule in Ireland through an acknowledged Protestant ascendancy - is today's survival of an anti-Catholic ethos within unionism. This is its predominant characteristic, and it varies only in degree - from plain dislike or contempt to a rabid and murderous hatred. Starkly and frightfully unique to loyalist terrorism has been the slaughter of Catholics just because they are Catholics. Fake alibis cannot mitigate that irrational rage. Loyalist killers themselves have described their activities as 'Taig-spraying'. The first murders in the recent epoch of troubles were of innocent Catholics who wandered into loyalist areas. Who can recall without a sense of appalling revulsion the horror of the UDA 'Romper Room' on the Shankill Road and the frightful torturing to death there of innocent 'Taigs' by the Shankill Butchers?

Possessed, therefore, of something similar to pure race hatred or anti-semitism, it is not surprising that some loyalist groups have recognised their political kith and kin abroad among extreme right-wing regimes and neo-nazi movements. They have had friendly contacts with Afrikaner racists in the former apartheid South Africa (where hate-imbued whites were also wont to go on black killing sprees), with the Ian Smith racists in former Rhodesia, and with the British National Front and right-wing extremists in Europe. It is understandable enough, then, that people whose minds are conditioned by that sort of outlook should often seem to have no politics at all. Being obsessed only with a consciousness of their different religion, they appear incapable of grasping what is involved in real political issues.

Yet unionist spokesmen throughout the spectrum continue to appropriate and twist current political terminology in a way that shows they have no real understanding of it. Self-determination and sovereignty are the buzz-words in the current debate, and unionists are using them with happy abandon, in typical copycat fashion, without even a remote idea of what they mean. They demand that their 'sovereignty' should not be encroached upon by the Dublin government, and insist upon the 'right to self-determination' of the Protestant and unionist people.

It takes a great deal of fantastic imagination - and unionist apologists have loads of it - to suppose that the Northern Ireland Protestants ever had any degree of sovereignty or self-determination over their own affairs even under the old Stormont regime. Absolute sovereignty has rested at Westminster, and the Stormont parliament had no more rights of self-determination than an English county council. The right to self-determination is an internationally recognised democratic right. Self-determination itself involves the ability to legislate for the common good and to exercise independent political powers over all matters of practical consequence for the community which possesses it. It would be an absurd contradiction to suggest that there can exist a 'right of self-determination' for a religious group in a community to thwart all moves towards self-determination for both themselves and for everyone else. The point can be clearly illustrated by taking a simple instance.

The British government had a plan to enrich the West-minster exchequer by stealing the water supplies belonging to the Northern Ireland people and selling them off to the financial robber barons of the City of London, who would then make enormous profits by selling the water back to the people who, rich and poor alike, would have to pay through the nose for every drop they consumed. Such a plundering of community resources would be, not only unlikely, but actually impossible under conditions of Irish sovereignty and self-determination, or even under any other interim arrangement which would allow the people of Northern Ireland to share some degree of sovereignty with the rest of the Irish people. However, if any British government should proceed with that plan, there is nothing anyone in Northern Ireland can do to stop it. We have no sovereign powers to prevent it, nor the slightest degree of self-determination to assert our inalienable right to what belongs to us. Here we see a tangible meaning to the terms 'birthright' and 'heritage'. The politicians who are betraying those things are the unionist politicians who uphold a relationship with Britain that makes a theft of that magnitude possible.

Realistic concerns like that - for there are others - serve to underline the fact that the people of Northern Ireland share a very immediate identity of interest. Issues of that sort should be engaging the attention of those working class groups who still call themselves 'loyalist', but who are moving away from traditional unionism - that is, if they really wish to advance the interests of their people. They can only relegate themselves to limbo in pursuit of a lost cause if they cling to a sectarian political Protestantism and archaic symbols like royal crowns and feudal regalia. The old six-county shape of things is now untenable.

What is needed is a conscious commitment to finding the means most conducive to allowing people gradually adapt to the coming changes - to a changed political climate and changed political arrangements and institutions. Even at a very simple level, for example, why should not local television stations be encouraged to produce a kind of soap opera in which friendly relations between the two religious communities are portrayed as normal, and in which sectarian prejudices are deprecated? There already are some hopeful signs of progress in that direction. The UTV programme, *Live at Six*, is notable for its cultural balance. We have come a long way since, before the troubles, a UTV programme called *Teatime with Tommy* was nicknamed 'Taig Time with Tommy' by sectarian bigots who resented the fact that the host and pianist, Tommy, was either a Catholic himself or gave time to Catholic singers and Irish dancers.

More than that is needed, of course. For instance, the moulders of opinion could stop producing aetiological fables which grant illusionary 'natural' origins to a separate Protestant identity, and the pseudo-intellectual material which does little more than provide feeding stuff for fanatics. The bi-centenary of the 1798 rebellion gives us an opportunity, if pursued with sense and discretion, to advance to its proper place in folk memory the healthier and more positive tradition that the Protestant people inherit from those times. Fortunately, we already have an excellent guide to help in that objective. It is the work of the late Dr Flann Campbell, published in 1991 and entitled *The Dissenting Voice: Protestant Democracy in Ulster from Plantation to Partition,* which illuminates a history so long kept in the dark. It deserves a great deal more acclaim than was accorded it by obviously biased reviewers.

More than anything else, of course, is the need to persuade Britain to abandon its historical role in underpinning sectarian division. Britain must be seen to withdraw its support for one side - a support which, being assumed, serves only to bolster and perpetuate expectations of special privilege based upon the antediluvian 'contract' ideology. Given that, the last prop of sectarianism is pulled away, and the last hope of sectarian politicians is removed. A substantial proportion of ordinary, normal Protestants - released from the sectarian six-county cage in which they are now trapped - may be happy to rediscover the true common identity and heritage, the real common interests and the better common traditions which they share with every-one else in Ireland. They have nothing to lose but their delusions.[†]

[†] This essay is based on a paper given to the Desmond Greaves Summer School in 1994.

NOTES ON CONTRIBUTORS

(In regard to optional spellings, certain styles of punctuation, and use of capitalisation, italics and numerals, I have accepted variation throughout this book and according to an author's preference, but did require that usage be consistent within a chapter and the references relating thereto. *D. Ó C.*)

Daltún Ó Ceallaigh An Arts graduate of Trinity College Dublin and writer on historical and political affairs; in particular, author of the books *Labour, Nationalism and Irish Freedom* (1991), *Sovereign People or Crown Subjects? - the case for articles 2 and 3* (1993), *Britain and Ireland - Sovereignty and Nationality* (1996), *The Northern Ireland Crisis - Multi-party Talks and Models for a Settlement* (1997); and editor of and contributor to *Reconsiderations of Irish History and Culture* (1994); by profession, General Secretary of the Irish Federation of University Teachers.

A F O'Brien Statutory Lecturer in the Department of History, National University of Ireland, Cork; also a Fellow of the Royal Historical Society; specialises in political and economic change and development in Ireland, and in the general European context, in the period 1169-1550.

Breandán Ó Buachalla MA, PhD, MRIA; Professor, Dublin Instiute for Advanced Studies (1973-8); Professor of Modern Irish Language and Literature, UCD (1978-96); Visiting Professor, New York University (1997); Parnell Fellow in Irish Studies, Magdalene College, University of Cambridge (1998); author of *I mBéal Feirste Cois Cuain* (1968), *Peadar Ó Doirnín: Amhráin* (1969), *Nua-Duanaire II* (1975), *Cathal Buí: Amhráin* (1976), *Aisling Ghéar* (1996), *An Caoineagus an Chaointeoireacht* (1998).

Brendan Bradshaw A graduate of UCD and a Marist priest; Director of Studies in History at Queens' College, Cambridge; Lecturer in History at the University; also a Fellow of the Royal Historical Society.

Roy Johnston A graduate in physics and mathematics from TCD; did PhD in the high-energy particle domain based on work at the École Polytechnique (Paris) and the Dublin Institute for Advanced Studies; subsequently went into industrial applied science; then became associated with the first major national computer project with Aer Lingus; since 1970, has been working as an applied science consultant and has written on various aspects of science and government; in particular was Science and Technology Correspondent for *The Irish Times* from 1970 to 1976; has also written a biographical piece on the Irish scientist J D Bernal covering the formative years up to 1922 (shortly to be published by Verso); currently working with the RDS on a Boyle Medal centenary monograph.

Anthony Coughlan Senior Lecturer in Social Policy at Trinity College, Dublin; Secretary of the National Platform organisation; and a member of the committee of the Desmond Greaves Summer School.

Jack Bennett Journalist and political commentator; author of several pamphlets on Northern affairs; foundation member of the Northern Ireland Civil rights Association; contributed for many years the 'Six County Commentary' to *The Sunday Press* under the pen name of Claud Gordon.

CHAPTER 1 - REFERENCES & NOTES

1. A Simms, 'Core and periphery in medieval Europe: the Irish experience in a wider context', in W J Smyth and K Whelan (eds), *Common Ground: Essays on the Historical Geography of Ireland* (Cork, 1988), pp 22-40:22.
2. *Ibid.*
3. R Bartlett, *The Making of Europe: Conquest, Colonization and Cultural Change 950-1350* (London, 1993), pp 306-7.
4. *Ibid*, p 51.
5. R R Davies, 'Lordship or colony?', in J F Lydon (ed), *The English in Medieval Ireland* (Dublin, Royal Irish Academy, 1984), p 151.
6. Simms, 'Core and periphery', pp 22-4.
7. W R Jones, 'England against the Celtic fringe: a study in cultural stereotypes', *Journal of World History*, xiii (1971), pp 155-171:159.
8. J Gillingham, 'The beginnings of English imperialism', *Journal of Historical Sociology*, v (1992), pp 392-409: 405-6. See also his 'The English invasion of Ireland', in B Bradshaw *et al.* (eds), *Representing Ireland: Literature and the Origins of Conflict 1534-1660* (Cambridge, 1993), pp 24-42, in which it is argued that the term 'English' is the appropriate one for the invaders of Ireland in the late twelfth and thirteenth centuries.
9. Gillingham, 'English imperialism', pp 405-6; 'English invasion', pp 393-8
10. R R Davies, *Domination and Conquest: The Experience of Ireland, Scotland and Wales 1100-1300* (Cambridge, 1990), pp 20-23
11. Gillingham, 'English imperialism', pp 405-6.
12. Jones, 'England against the Celtic fringe', pp 155-6.
13. Gillingham, 'English imperialism', pp 402-3. See also Bartlett, *The Making of Europe*, pp 76-7.
14. Davies, *Domination and Conquest*, pp 9-10.
15. Jones, 'England against the Celtic fringe', p 157.
16. Gillingham, 'English imperialism', pp 403-5.
17. *Ibid.*
18. Jones, 'England against the Celtic fringe', pp 166-7.
19. Bartlett, *The Making of Europe*, pp 22-3.
20. *Ibid*, p 21.

21. Gillingham, 'English imperialism', p 401.
22. Gillingham, 'English invasion', p 24.
23. Simms, 'Core and periphery', p 23.
24. J J O'Meara (ed), *Gerald of Wales: the History and Topography of Ireland* (Harmondsworth, 1982), p 12.
25. *Ibid*, p 14.
26. Bartlett, *The Making of Europe*, p 97. See also A B Scott and F X Martin (eds), *Expugnatio Hibernica* (Dublin, 1978).
27. Jones, 'England against the Celtic fringe', p 160.
28. R Frame, *The Political Development of the British Isles 1100-1400* (2nd edn, Oxford, 1995), p 187.
29. Davies, *Domination and Conquest*, p 77.
30. *Ibid*, pp 83-4; 'Lordship or colony?', p 160.
31. C A Empey, 'Conquest and settlement: patterns of Anglo-Norman settlement in north Munster and south Leinster', *Irish Economic and Social History*, xiii (1986), pp 5-31:5.
32. R Davies, 'Frontier arrangements in fragmented societies: Ireland and Wales', in R Bartlett and A MacKay (eds), *Medieval Frontier Societies* (Oxford, 1992), pp 77-100:79.
33. *Ibid*. For the question of the frontier in later medieval Ireland, see also J F Lydon, 'The problem of the frontier in medieval Ireland', *Topic: A Journal of the Liberal Arts*, 13 (1967), pp 5-22.
34. See, for example, A F O'Brien, 'Episcopal elections in Ireland *c* 1254-72', *Proceedings of the Royal Irish Academy*, C, lxxiii (1973), pp 129-76.
35. Empey, 'Conquest and settlement', p 5.
36. *Ibid*, p 8.
37. Davies, *Domination and Conquest*, pp 99-103.
38. Davies, 'Lordship or colony?', pp 151-8.
39. K W Nicholls, 'Anglo-French Ireland and after', *Peritia*, i (1982), pp 370-403:371.
40. Davies, 'Lordship or colony?', pp 151-8.
41. *Ibid*.
42. Bartlett, *The Making of Europe*, pp 225-6.
43. O'Brien, 'Episcopal elections', p 131. See also J A Watt, *The Church and the Two Nations in Medieval Ireland* (Cambridge, 1970).
44. Davies, 'Lordship or colony?', p 153.
45. Bartlett, *The Making of Europe*, pp 238-9.

46. ' ... if ony man duellyng [= dwelling] within the lyberte of the same citie [Waterford] shal curse, diffame, or dispice ony citsayn of the saide citie in calling him Yrishman, and herupon he shal be convicted and shal gyve to him xiii s. iiii d. ... ' (J T Gilbert, 'Archives of the municipal corporation of Waterford' in *Historical Manuscripts Commission, Tenth Report, Appendix, Part V* (London, 1885), p 292.

47. ' ... it was ordayned that no manere of man of Yrishe blood nether bondman be recevid unto the fredome of the saide citie [Waterford] withoute he have his fredome and liberte of the Kynge afor and of the lorde that he is bonde unto' (*ibid*, pp 299-300). Similarly, in 1470, 'it was ordayned and enactid ... that no man be recevid marchaunt [= merchant] of the Staple, lasse than afor [= unless that previously] he be a freman sworne of the saide citie and of Inglish nacion, or else to have his liberte of the Kyng ... ' (*ibid*, p 306).

48. *Ibid*, p 303.

49. *Ibid*, pp 307-8.

50. For what follows, see A F O'Brien 'Politics, economy and society: the development of Cork and the Irish south-coast region *c* 1170 to *c* 1583' in P O'Flanagan and C G Buttimer (eds), *Cork: History and Society: Interdisciplinary Essays on the History of an Irish County,* pp 83-154: 133-5.

51. For grants of denization, or grants of English law made by the English crown to persons of the Irish nation, see G J Hand, 'The status of the native Irish in the lordship of Ireland 1272-1331' in *Irish Jurist* (1966), pp 93-115 and B Murphy, 'The status of the native Irish after 1331' in *Irish Jurist* (1967), pp 116-28.

52. Davies, *Domination and Conquest*, p 119.

53. K Simms, 'Bards and barons: the Anglo-Irish aristocracy and the native culture', in Bartlett and MacKay, *Frontier Societies,* pp 177-197:191.

54. *Ibid*, 196-7.

55. J F Lydon, 'The middle nation', in Lydon (ed), *The English in Medieval Ireland,* pp 1-26.

56. R Frame, ' "Les Engleys nées en Irlande": the English political identity in medieval Ireland', *Transactions of the Royal Historical Society*, sixth series, iii (1993), pp 83-103:96.

57. Nichols, 'Anglo-French Ireland', p 398.

58. This matter is examined in some detail in my 'The royal boroughs, the seaport towns and royal revenue in medieval Ireland', *Journal of the Royal Society of Antiquaries of Ireland*, cxviii (1988), pp 13-26. This matter is covered in some detail in my 'The royal boroughs, the seaport towns and royal revenue in medieval Ireland', *Journal of the Royal Society of Antiquaries of Ireland*, cxviii (1998), pp 13-26. See also my 'Irish exchequer records of payments of the fee farm of the city of Cork in the later middle ages', *Analecta Hibernica*, 37, pp 139-189.

59. W G Hoskins, *The Age of Plunder: The England of Henry VIII 1500-1547* (London, 1976), pp 207-11.

60. S G Ellis, *Tudor Ireland: Crown, Community and the Conflict of Cultures 1470-1603* (London, 1985), pp 14-15.

61. D B Quinn, 'Ireland and sixteenth-century European expansion', in T D Williams (ed), *Historical Studies I* (London, 1958), pp 22-32.

62. B Bradshaw, 'Native reaction to the westward enterprise: a case-study in Gaelic ideology', in K R Andrews *et al* (eds), *The Westward Enterprise: English Activities in Ireland, the Atlantic, and America 1480-1650* (Liverpool, 1978), pp 65-80:67.

63. C Brady, 'The decline of the Irish kingdom', in M Greengrass (ed.), *Conquest and Coalescence: The Shaping of the State in Early Modern Europe* (London, 1991), pp 94-115: 100.

64. C Brady, *The Chief Governors: The Rise and Fall of Reform Government in Tudor Ireland 1536-1588* (Cambridge, 1994), pp 52-3

65. *Ibid*, pp 94-7.

66. N Canny, *Kingdom and Colony: Ireland in the Atlantic World 1560-1800* (Baltimore, 1988), pp 5-6.

67. Brady, *The Chief Governors*, p 251.

68. N Canny, 'Irish, Scottish and Welsh responses to centralisation *c* 1530 – *c* 1640: a comparative perspective', in A Grant and K J Stringer (eds), *Uniting the Kingdom? The Making of British History* (London, 1995), pp 147-69:152. See also Canny, *Kingdom and Colony*, pp 2-5 and Brady, *The Chief Governors*, p 255.

69. Brady, *The Chief Governors*, p 255.

70. For the Munster and Ulster plantations, see M MacCarthy-Morrogh, *The Munster Plantation: English Migration to Southern Ireland 1583-1641* (Oxford, 1986) and P Robinson, *The Plantation of*

Ulster: British Settlement in an Irish Landscape 1600-1670 (2nd edn, Belfast, 1994).

71. Canny, *Kingdom and Colony,* pp 4-5.

72. N P Canny, 'The ideology of English colonization: from Ireland to America', *William and Mary Quarterly,* 3rd series, xxx(1973), pp 575-98: 593-5

73. *Ibid,* p 592.

74. Bartlett, *The Making of Europe,* p 99. For a comparison of the medieval and sixteenth-century situations, see Gillingham, 'English invasion'.

75. J Youings, 'Did Raleigh's England need colonies?', in J Youings (ed), *Raleigh in Exeter 1985: Privateering and Colonisation in the Reign of Elizabeth I* (Exeter, 1985), pp 39-57.

76. H A Mac Dougall, *Racial Myth in English History: Trojans, Teutons, and Anglo-Saxons* (Montreal, 1982), p 31.

77. *Ibid,* p 37.

78. R Davis, *The Rise of the Atlantic Economies* (London, 1973), p 228.

79. Canny, 'Ideology', p 589.

80. B Bradshaw, 'Robe and sword in the conquest of Ireland', in C Cross *et al.* (eds), *Law and Government under the Tudors* (Cambridge, 1988), pp 139-62: 162.

81. B Cunningham, 'Native culture and political change in Ireland 1580-1640', in C Brady and R Gillespie (eds), *Natives and Newcomers: Essays on the Making of Irish Colonial Society 1534-1641* (Dublin, 1986), pp 148-70.

82. Canny, 'Ideology', p 592.

83. *Ibid,* p 589.

84. *Ibid.*

85. *Ibid,* pp 586-7.

86. K S Bottigheimer, 'Kingdom and colony: Ireland in the westward enterprise 1536-1600', in Andrews *et al* (eds), *The Westward Enterprise,* pp 45-64:52.

87. Canny, 'Ideology', p 575.

88. *Ibid,* p 596. See also Bottigheimer, 'Kingdom and colony', p 59.

89. Canny, *Kingdom and Colony,* pp 36-7.

90. *Ibid,* p. 2.

91. N Canny, *The Elizabethan Conquest of Ireland: A Pattern Established 1565-76* (Hassocks, 1976), p 51.

92. N Canny, 'The permissive frontier: social control in English settlements in Ireland and Virginia, 1550-1650' in Andrews *et al* (eds), *The Westward Enterprise*, p 20.

93. Canny, *Kingdom and Colony*, p 28.

94. *Ibid*, p 29.

95. Bottigheimer, 'Kingdom and colony', p 55. Boyle's career in Ireland is described in T O Ranger, 'Richard Boyle and the making of an Irish fortune, 1588-1614', *Irish Historical Studies*, x (1957), pp 257-97 and in N P Canny, *The Upstart Earl: A Study of the Social and Mental World of Richard Boyle, First Earl of Cork, 1566-1643* (Cambridge, 1982).

96. Ranger, 'Richard Boyle', p 262.

97. *Ibid*, p 273.

98. Canny, *Kingdom and Colony*, pp 44-5.

99. *Ibid*, p 42.

100. *Ibid*, pp 44-5.

101. *Ibid*, p 40.

102. A F O'Brien, 'Commercial relations between Aquitaine and Ireland *c* 1000 to *c* 1550', in Jean-Michel Picard (ed), *Aquitaine and Ireland in the Middle Ages* (Dublin, 1995), pp 31-80: 73n 54.

103. O'Brien, 'Commercial relations', *passim.*

104. R Gillespie, 'Explorers, exploiters and entrepreneurs: early modern Ireland and its context, 1500-1700', in B J Graham and L J Proudfoot (eds), *An Historical Geography of Ireland* (London, 1993), pp 123-57:132.

105. Brady, *The Chief Governors*, p 128.

106. R Gillespie, *Colonial Ulster: The Settlement of East Ulster 1600-1641* (Cork, 1985), pp 13-14.

107. Canny, *Kingdom and Colony*, pp 52-3.

108. R Gillespie, *The Transformation of the Irish Economy 1550-1700* (Economic and Social History Society of Ireland, 1991), p 35.

109. O'Brien, 'Commercial relations', p 36. See also A K Longfield, *Anglo-Irish Trade in the Sixteenth Century* (London, 1929).

110. E McCracken, *The Irish Woods Since Tudor Times: Distribution and Exploitation* (Newton Abbot, 1971), p 98.

111. Canny, 'Permissive frontier', p. 20. Cf, for example, the role of Henry Oughtred a prominent Southampton merchant and shipowner (D B Quinn, 'The Munster Plantation: problems and opportunities', *Journal of the Cork Historical and Archaeological Society*, lxxxi, 1966, pp 19-40:25).

112. Canny, *Kingdom and Colony*, pp 52-3.

113. Gillespie, *Transformation*, p 34.

114. Gillespie, *Colonial Ulster*, p 14.

115. Mc Cracken, *Irish Woods*, p 105.

116. *Ibid*, p 100.

117. Canny, *Kingdom and Colony*, pp 52-3.

118. Bottigheimer, 'Kingdom and colony', p 46.

119. Quinn, 'Ireland and European expansion', p 22.

120. Quinn, 'Munster Plantation', p 21.

121. *Ibid*, p 30.

122. Hoskins, *Age of Plunder*, p 220. See also Davis, *Atlantic Economies*, pp 194-211.

123. Davis, *Atlantic Economies*, p 194.

124. O'Brien, 'Politics, economy and society', p 118.

125. Davis, *Atlantic Economies*, p 209.

126. N P Canny, *The Formation of the Old English Elite in Ireland* (NUI, O'Donnell Lecture, 1974), pp 17-18.

127. Davis, *Atlantic Economies*, p 76.

128. H Morgan, 'The colonial venture of Sir Thomas Smith in Ulster, 1571-1575', *The Historical Journal*, xxviii (1985), pp 261-278:261.

129. *Ibid*, p 269.

130. *Ibid*.

131. *Ibid*, p 270.

132. Davis, *Atlantic Economies*, pp 77-8.

133. *Ibid*, p 83.

134. *Ibid*, p 238.

135. *Ibid*, pp 80-82.

136. Canny, 'Ideology', p 596.

137. Quinn, 'Munster Plantation', pp 24-5.

138. *Ibid*.

139. *Ibid*, p 32; Canny, 'Permissive frontier', pp 42-3.

140. Canny, 'Ideology', p 596.

141. A Clarke, 'The Irish economy, 1600-60', in T W. Moody *et al* (eds), *A New History of Ireland. iii. Early Modern Ireland 1534-1691* (Oxford, 1976), pp 168-86:169.

142. L M Cullen, *An Economic History of Ireland Since 1660* (2nd edn, London, 1987), p 9.

143. Bottigheimer, 'Kingdom and colony', p 63.